1B

World Class

EXPANDING ENGLISH FLUENCY

NANCY DOUGLAS | JAMES R. MORGAN

NATIONAL GEOGRAPHIC LEARNING | CENGAGE Learning®

Australia • Brazil • Japan • Korea • Mexico • Singapore • Spain • United Kingdom • United States

NATIONAL GEOGRAPHIC LEARNING | CENGAGE Learning

World Class: Expanding English Fluency
Student Edition

Nancy Douglas and James R. Morgan

Publisher: Sherrise Roehr

Managing Editor: Sarah Thérèse Kenney

Development Editors: Michael Poor, Michael Tom

Senior Technology Product Manager: Scott Rule

Technology Project Manager: Chris Conroy

Director of Global Marketing: Ian Martin

Senior Product Marketing Manager: Katie Kelley

Director, Content and Media Production: Michael Burggren

Content Project Manager: Andrea Bobotas

Print Buyer: Mary Beth Hennebury

Cover Designer: Cenveo Publisher Services

Cover Image: Jeff Curtes

Compositor: Cenveo Publisher Services

Student Book + Student CD-ROM ISBN: 978-1-133-31081-5
Student Book + Online Workbook ISBN: 978-1-285-06309-6
Combo Split 1B + Student CD-ROM ISBN: 978-1-133-56588-8
Combo Split 1B + Online Workbook ISBN: 978-1-285-41988-6

National Geographic Learning
20 Channel Center Street
Boston, MA 02210
USA

Cengage Learning is a leading provider of customized learning solutions with office locations around the globe, including Singapore, the United Kingdom, Australia, Mexico, Brazil and Japan.

Cengage Learning products are represented in Canada by Nelson Education, Ltd.

Visit National Geographic Learning online at **ngl.cengage.com**

Visit our corporate website at **www.cengage.com**

Photo Credits

Unit 7 pp.72–73: Tino Soriano/National Geographic Stock; **p.74**, top: Mika Heittola/Shutterstock.com; bottom: Ira Block/National Geographic Stock; **p.76**: Yusef El-Mansouri/Shutterstock.com; **p.78**, top: Rohan Van Twest/Alamy; bottom left: Supri Suharjoto/Shutterstock.com; bottom right: Kzenon/Shutterstock.com; **p.80**: ©iStockphoto.com/Henrik Jonsson; **p.81**: Morgan Lane Photography/Shutterstock.com; **p.82**: Katrina Brown/Dreamstime.com; **p.83**: David Cupp/National Geographic Stock

Unit 8 pp.84–85: Keith Barraclough/National Geographic Stock; **p.86**: Dirk Anschütz/Corbis; **p.87**: Mike Theiss/National Geographic Stock; **p.88**, top: William Weems/National Geographic Stock; bottom: Catalin Petolea/Shutterstock.com; **p.89**: Mika/Corbis; **p.93**, top: Image Source/Corbis; bottom: Dmytro Konstantynov/Dreamstime.com; **p. 94**, top: Cristi_m/Dreamstime.com; middle: Benoit Tessier/Reuters/Corbis; bottom: StockLite/Shutterstock.com; **p.95**, left: Caro/Alamy; right: Ianni Dimitrov/Alamy

Unit 9 pp.96–97: Patrick Shyu/National Geographic Stock; **p.98**: Jmiks/Shutterstock.com; **p.100**, top: Richard Laschon/Shutterstock.com; middle: donatas1205/Shutterstock.com; bottom: Vincent J. Musi/National Geographic Stock; **p.101**: John Elk III/Alamy; **p.102**: Gary Roberts/Alamy; **p.103**: Michael Nichols/National Geographic Stock; **p.105**, top: Konrad Wothe/Minden Pictures; middle: Medford Taylor/National Geographic Stock; bottom: Shawnjackson/Dreamstime.com; **p.106**: Renate Micallef/Dreamstime.com; **p.107**: Picsfive/Shutterstock.com

Unit 10 pp.108–109: Jim Richardson/National Geographic Stock; **p.110**, left (top): Gelpi/Shutterstock.com; (bottom): Chris Rout/Alamy; right: Peter Zoeller/Design Pics/Corbis; **p.111**: Sandra Eckhardt/Corbis; **p.113**: James Woodson/Thinkstock; **p.114**: takito/Shutterstock.com; **p.115**: Chris Crisman/Corbis; **p.116**: auremar/Shutterstock.com; **p.117**: MedusArt/Shutterstock.com; **p.118**: Nik Wheeler/Corbis

Unit 11 pp.120–121: Sigurdur Hrafn Stefnisson; **p.122**, top: Reuters/Corbis; bottom: George F. Mobley/National Geographic Stock; **p.123**: AFP/Getty Images; **p.124**: John Lund/Drew Kelly/Blend Images/Corbis; **p.125**, left to right: Jack Reynolds/Getty Images; Brian Thompson/National Geographic Stock; Mike Theiss/National Geographic Stock; **p.126**, top: Czacio/Dreamstime.com; bottom: John Wollwerth/Dreamstime.com; **p.127**: Chris Collins/Corbis; **p.128**: Kristina Afanasyeva/Dreamstime.com; **p.129**: Jim Reed/Jim Reed Photography - Severe & /Corbis; **p.130**: Sam Kittner/National Geographic Stock

Unit 12 pp.132–133: Chuck Pefley/Alamy; **p.134**, top: Jonathan Larsen/Diadem Images/Alamy; bottom: Jason Swalwell/Shutterstock.com; **p.135**: Shelly Castellano/Icon SMI/Corbis; **p.136**, top: Vico Collective/Alin Dragulin/Blend Images/Corbis; bottom: new vave/Shutterstock.com; **p.137**: Seandnad/Dreamstime.com; **pp.138–139**: Fritz Hoffmann/National Geographic Stock; **p.139**: John Warburton-Lee Photography/Alamy; **p.140**: Ang Wee Heng John/Dreamstime.com; **p.141**. Myrleen Pearson/Alamy; **p.143**: Ben Radford/Corbis

Text Credits

Readings from the following units were adapted from National Geographic.

Unit 7 Adapted from *Changing America* by Joel L. Swerdlow, National Geographic Magazine, September 2001. **Unit 9** Adapted from *Orphans No More* by Charles Siebert, National Geographic Online, September 2011. **Unit 10** Adapted from *Beautiful Brains* by David Dobbs, National Geographic Magazine, October 2011. **Unit 12** Adapted from *Battle for the Soul of Kung Fu* by Peter Gwin, National Geographic Magazine, March 2011.

Printed in China
3 4 5 6 7 18 17 16 15

Acknowledgements

The authors and editorial team would like to thank the many dedicated instructors who took the time to review World Class. *Their feedback was invaluable during the development of this program.*

UNITED STATES Touria Ghaffari, EC New York, New York, New York; **Olga Gusak,** Computer Systems Institute, Skokie, Illinois; **William Jex,** American Language Institute, New York University, New York, New York; **Bridget McDonald,** Independent Learning Services, Boston, Massachusetts; **Saida Pagan,** North Valley OC, Mission Hills, California; **Tara Tarpey,** American Language Institute, New York University, New York, New York

LATIN AMERICA Luiz Otávio Barros, Associação Alumni, Brazil; **Clarissa Bezerra,** Casa Thomas Jefferson, Brazil; **Isabela Villas Boas,** Casa Thomas Jefferson, Brazil; **Tatiane C. de Carvalho,** Cultura Britânica e Americana, Brazil; **Rafael Reis Carpanez,** Cultura Inglesa, Brazil; **Janette Carvalhinho de Oliveira,** Centro de Linguas - UFES, Brazil; **Samara Camilo Tomé Costa,** IBEU, Brazil; **Frank Couto,** Casa Thomas Jefferson, Brazil; **Denise Santos da Silva,** Associação Cultural Estados Unidos, Brazil; **Marilena Fernandes,** Associação Alumni, Brazil; **Vanessa Ferreira,** Associação Cultural Brasil Estados Unidos, Brazil; **Marcia Ferreira,** CCBEU Franca, Brazil; **Maria Regina Filgueiras,** College Language Center, Brazil; **Maria Righini,** Associação Cultura Inglesa, Brazil; **Bebeth Silva Costa,** Betina's English Course, Brazil; **Domingos Sávio Siqueira,** Federal University of Bahia, Brazil; **Joyce von Söhsten,** English by Joyce von Söhsten, Brazil; **Doris Flores,** Universidad Santo Tomas, Chile; **Sandra Herrera,** Inacap Apoquindo, Chile; **Jair Ayala Zarate,** La Salle University, Colombia; **Rosario Mena,** Instituto Cultural Dominico Americano, Dominican Republic; **Raúl Billini,** Language Program Administration, Dominican Republic; **Rosa Vásquez,** John F. Kennedy Institute of Languages, INC., Dominican Republic; **Elizabeth Ortiz,** COPEI-COPOL English Institute, Ecuador; **José Alonso Gaxiola Soto,** Universidad Autonoma de Sinaloa, Mexico; **María Elena Mesías Ratto,** Universidad de San Martín de Porres, Peru

EUROPE AND THE MIDDLE EAST Juan Irigoyen, International Institute, Spain; **Nashwa Nashaat Sobhy,** San Jorge University, Spain; **Barbara Van der Veer,** International Institute, Spain **Deborah Wilson,** American University of Sharjah, United Arab Emirates

ASIA Michael Lay, American Intercon Institute, Cambodia; **Kirkland Arizona Kenney,** Beijing New Oriental School, China; **Isao Akama,** Waseda University, Japan; **Benjamin Bailey,** University of Shizuoka, Japan; **James Baldwin,** Toyko University of Agriculture and Technology, Japan; **Jonathan deHaan,** University of Shizuoka, Japan; **Todd Enslen,** Tohoku University, Japan; **Peter Gray,** Hokusei Gakuen University, Japan; **Linda Hausman,** Gakushuin University, Japan; **Mauro Lo Dico,** Nanzan University, Japan; **Nobue Mori,** Kumamoto Gakuen University, Japan; **Yuri Nishio,** Gifu Pharmaceutical University, Japan; **Geraldine Norris,** The Prefectual University of Shizuoka, Japan; **Christopher Piper,** Takushoku University, Japan; **Michael Radcliffe,** Yokohama City University, Japan; **Jean-Pierre Richard,** Kanagawa University, Sophia University, Japan; **Greg Rouault,** Konan University, Hirao School of Management, Japan; **Stephen Ryan,** Yamagata University, Japan; **Gregory Strong,** Aoyama Gakuin University, Japan; **Michael Yasui,** Tokyo Metropolitan University, Japan; **Sun Mi Ma,** Ajou University, Korea; **Palarak Chaiyo,** Rajamangala University of Technology Suvarnabhumi, Thailand; **Krishna Kosashunhanan,** Thai-Nichai Institute of Technology, Thailand; **Jonee de Leon,** Universal English Center, Vietnam; **Ai Nguyen Huynh Thi,** VUS, Vietnam

We would also like to extend a special thank-you to Yeny Kim for her many insights. Her thoughtful contributions were a great asset and will be felt by students and teachers alike.

UNIT	VOCABULARY	GRAMMAR	LISTENING
UNIT 7  On the Move, 72	Advice on how to get around your city	Comparative Forms	A Commuter's Diary **Strategy:** Listening for connections between ideas
UNIT 8  Think Twice, 84	Text messaging during class	Past Modals	Problems with posting online **Strategy:** Determining a speaker's attitude **Pronunciation:** Reduction with past modals
UNIT 9  In the Wild, 96	Three of our favorite pets	Review of Passive Voice	Bonobos: Humans' closest relative **Strategy:** Detecting uncertainty
UNIT 10 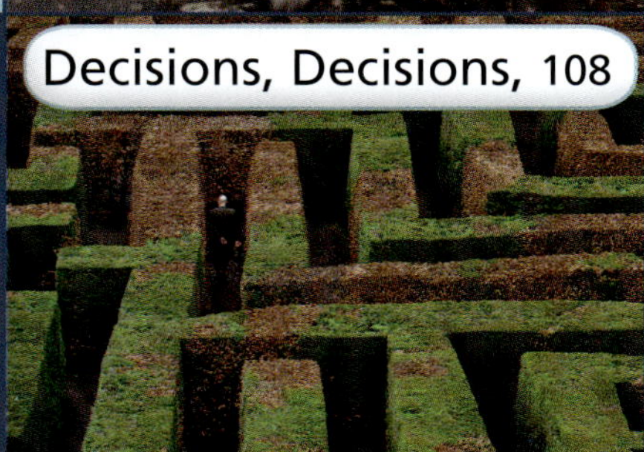 Decisions, Decisions, 108	Brain teaser: What do you know about the brain and decision making	The Conditional	Three everyday decisions
UNIT 11  Rain or Shine, 120	Bad weather traps doctor on the South Pole	Phrasal Verbs	Reactions to the weather
UNIT 12  What's Your Game, 132	Favorite sports	Reported Speech	An interview with a professional athlete

READING	WRITING	SPEAKING	VIDEO
One Foot on The Gas: Children of immigrants discover American car culture	Write a letter of complaint	Consider the facts in an immigration case **Strategy:** Presenting facts and announcing a decision	*Capital Bikeshare*
Nowhere to Hide: What happens when our private lives become public	Give an opinion on an event **Strategy:** Writing an effective online post	Evaluate different surveillance practices	*Protecting reputations online*
Orphan Elephants: A center in Kenya rescues, rehabilitates and researches baby elephants	Write an informational brochure **Strategy:** Getting the reader's attention	Debate what to do about three animals at risk	*Great Migrations* (excerpt)
The Teenage Brain: Why teenagers act the way they do **Strategy:** Recognizing cause and effect	Use cause and effect to explain a decision you'd make **Strategy:** Showing cause and effect	Analyze how you handle peer pressure	*Moral Dilemma* (excerpt): **Pronunciation:** Thought groups
Storm Chasers: Scientists risk their lives to gather data about tornadoes **Strategy:** Making inferences	Describe a time weather impacted your life **Strategy:** Include figurative language	Which weather story is false?	*Sinking England*
The Spirit of Kung Fu: A Shaolin master faces the world of kung fu	Write about important qualities **Strategy:** Writing a timed essay	Present an activity **Strategy:** Speaking from an outline	Alain Robert, "*The French Spiderman*"

Explore a Unit

The first half of each unit leads students through guided and communicative practice to master target structures.

Clearly stated **Unit Outcomes** provide a roadmap of learning for the student.

Stunning images and thought-provoking questions encourage learners to **think critically** about the unit theme.

Relevant, high frequency vocabulary is practiced in contextualized exercises.

Pronunciation boxes offer support and tips as well as cross reference to full explanation and practice in the appendix.

The **Grammar** section allows learners to refine their grammar skills and practice the grammar through first controlled and then open-ended activities.

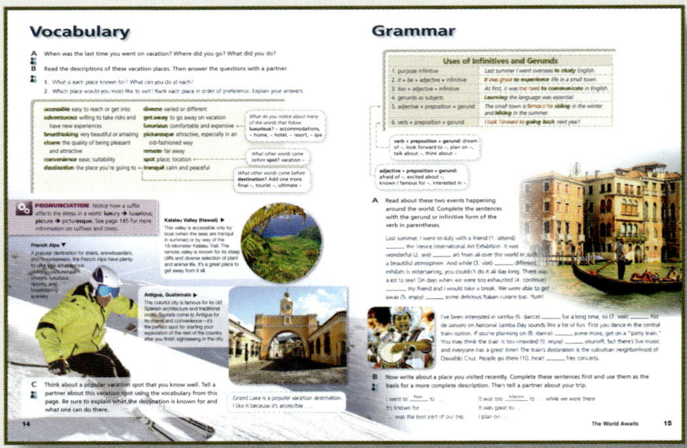

Listening activities encourage learners to listen for and consolidate key information, reinforcing the language, and allowing learners to personalize and think critically about the information they hear.

The **Connections** section allows learners to synthesize the vocabulary and grammar they have learned through personalized communication.

The second half of the unit focuses on skill-building and communication. The strands build on one another with a final communicative task before Expanding Your Fluency. For this reason, the order of strands may vary from unit to unit.

Learners navigate **interesting and relevant readings** from National Geographic through pre-, while-, and post-reading activities,helping them to comprehend the main idea and key details of the passage.

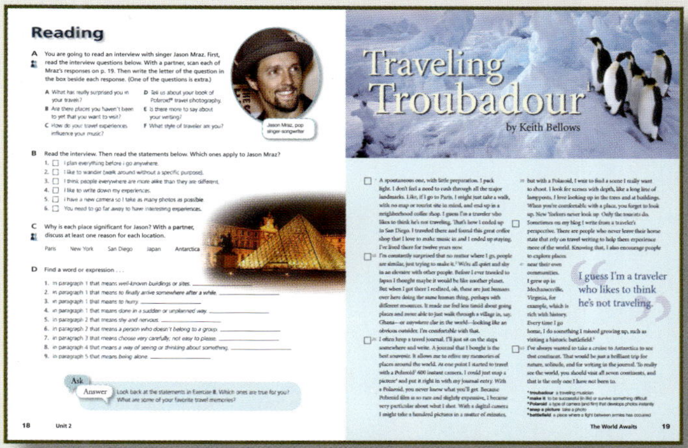

Learners are encouraged to perform **Speaking** tasks in pairs and groups. Where appropriate, **strategies** are provided to ensure students' successful communication.

The **Video** section brings the world into the classroom with authentic clips, including news stories, PSAs, and National Geographic documentaries.

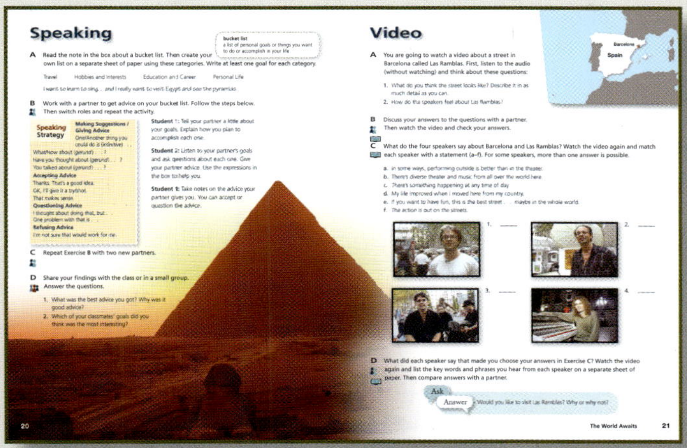

The **Writing** section includes writing models to prompt learners to complete a functional piece of writing and also serves as a culminating activity in many units.

The **Expanding Your Fluency** section allows learners to apply the language they have learned throughout the unit in real-world tasks and offers self-assessment checks.

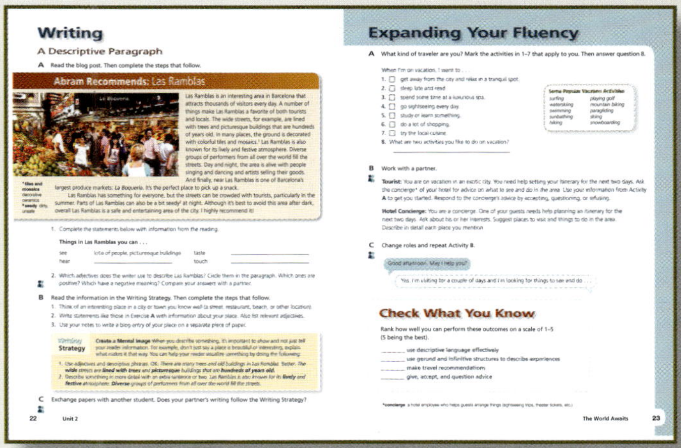

7 On the Move

1 What do you think of when you hear the expression "on the move" (traveling to school or work, taking a trip, moving to a new place, or something else)?

2 Look at the photo and imagine the people that are traveling. Who are these people and where are they going? Why do you think they're on the move?

3 What's the most routine trip you take? What's the biggest trip you've ever taken?

Unit Outcomes

In this unit, you will learn to:

- make comparisons
- recognize cause-and-effect relationships
- make a complaint and propose a solution
- use facts and evidence to defend a position

Vocabulary

A How do people get around where you live—by bike, car, train? Make a list of all the modes of transportation (including walking). Then answer these questions with a partner.

Which mode of transportation is best when you . . .

1. are going to work or school?
2. want to take a long trip?
3. don't have a lot of money?

commute the daily journey you make between your home and work or school
cramped not big enough for the number of people or things in it
delay when you have to wait longer than expected for something to happen
fit in to feel that you belong to a particular group and are accepted by them
keep in mind to remember something important (often a warning / advice)
option something you can choose from a group of alternatives
overwhelming difficult to fight against
punctual on time; not late
reliable trusted to work or behave well
rush hour the times of day when most people are traveling to and from work
tend likely to behave in a particular way
transfer to go or move something from one place to another

Other expressions with *keep: ~ your promise/ word, ~ an appointment, ~ a secret, ~ up*

B Read Vanessa's tips about getting around her city. Use words from the list above to complete her advice.

Getting around a big city can be (1) __________. There are so many transportation (2) __________ that it's hard to know which one to choose. Here's my advice. When you have to travel a long distance, think twice before getting into a taxi. They can be expensive, and heavy traffic can result in frequent (3) __________. Take the subway instead. It may not always be (4) __________, but it's reasonably priced, clean, and reliable. You should (5) __________, though, that most locals use the subway to commute to and from work or school. Allow extra time if you have several transfers to make. If you don't like cramped spaces, it's best to avoid the subway during (6) __________. For short trips, you can simply walk to your destination. If you do all these things, you'll fit in just like a local!

C How does your city or town compare to Vanessa's? Work with a partner to complete these sentences.

1. When you have to go a long distance, you should . . .
2. For short trips, it's best to . . .
3. When it comes to commuting, most locals . . .
4. The best way to avoid delays is to . . .
5. The most important thing to keep in mind is . . .

Grammar

A Compared to five years ago, which of these sentences describes rush hour in your city or town today? Complete the sentences with the correct comparative form of *convenient*. Then choose an answer.

a. It's ________________ to get around than it was before. (It's better.)

b. It's ________________ than it was before. (It's worse.)

c. It's about the same.

TIP We don't usually use *less* with one-syllable adjectives. We use *not as . . . as* instead. ~~*The bus is less fast than the train*~~. *The bus is not as fast as the train.*

Comparative Forms			
	more than . . .	**less than . . .**	**equal to . . .**
Adjectives	Taking a taxi is **faster** and **more reliable than** taking the subway.	The subways are **less reliable than** they used to be. They are **not as nice as** they once were.	During rush hour, walking is **as fast as** taking the bus.
Adverbs	The trains run **faster** and **more frequently** than the bus.	The trains run **less frequently** on weekends than they do on weekdays.	The old trains run **as smoothly as** the new ones.
Noncount nouns	After I quit, I had **more time than** I used to.	As a new parent, I have **less time than** I used to.	I spend **as much** time working **as** (I did) before.
Count nouns	The local train makes **more stops than** the express (does).	The express train makes **fewer stops than** the local (does).	The Blue Line has **as many riders** as it did last year.
Irregular forms: good → better, bad → worse, far → further			

B Make sentences comparing these two subway lines. Which would you prefer to ride?

	Blue Line	**Green Line**
number of riders	140,000 per month	100,000 per month
train tracks	2 years old	15 years old
daily schedule	weekdays: every 5 minutes weekend: every 16 minutes	weekdays: every 5 minutes weekends: every 12 minutes
on time schedule	arrives late 8% of the time	arrives late 2% of the time
cleanliness	moderately clean	very clean
hear the announcements	clear 97% of the time	clear 82% of the time

C You are going to talk about the best way to travel between two points. Work with a group.

1. Choose a starting point and an ending point in a place you know well. The points should be far enough apart to require a combination of public transportation, driving, or walking to get there.
2. Think of two different routes you could take to get to your final destination.
3. Compare the pros and cons of the two routes using comparative language.

Listening

get in arrive
pull in / pull out arrive / depart (especially used for vehicles such as trains, trucks, and cars)

A Look at the photo below. How long is your typical commute to school or work?

B Listen to a news broadcast in which the reporter, Jeremy Wexler, talks about his commute. As you listen, mark the correct answer for each item.

1. The average commuting time is **increasing / decreasing**.
2. Jeremy probably lives in **the suburbs / the city**.
3. It is **common / not common** for the 8:12 train to be late.
4. His office is **near / far from** the train station.
5. He's probably **sitting / standing** on the train.
6. Jeremy takes **one train / more than one train** to work.

Listening Strategy

Connecting ideas Listen for expressions like these that connect ideas. They show a cause-and-effect relationship between one idea and another: *As a result . . . / Because of that . . . / That means that . . . / When that happens . . .*

C Read the Listening Strategy. Then listen again. Mark your answers to show the cause-and-effect relationships that Jeremy describes.

1. The trains are **older / newer**. → They break down **more / less** often. → They run **more / less** frequently. → People are **more / less** likely to find a seat.
2. The stations are **cleaner / not as clean**. → The commute is **more / less** pleasant.
3. Traffic is **better / worse** these days. → Commuting by car is **slower / faster**.

Ask Answer Central Station seems to be the busiest commuting hub in Jeremy's city. What about your city or town? What is the busiest center for transportation? How does it compare to Central Station?

Video

availability the fact that something can be used or reached
bottom line the total amount of money a company has made or lost over a particular amount of time
perfect match two things that go or work together successfully

A Read about bikeshare programs. Is there anything like this where you live?

Bikeshare programs provide bicycles for public use as an alternative to driving or taking public transportation. For a small fee, individuals can join the program and use the bicycles for short trips around the city. There are currently about two hundred bikeshare programs worldwide.

Word Partnership

Look at the verbs in blue. What do they mean? Use your dictionary to help you.

I use bikeshare to **get around** town.

I **get on** the bike near the station and **drop** it **off** ten minutes later.

I use bikeshare when I have to **pick up** my son at school.

B Washington, DC is the capital of the United States. The city has a bikeshare program. Follow these steps.

a. Read through items 1–6 below. Can you guess any of the answers?
b. Watch the video once. Don't write anything.
c. Watch again and complete the sentences.

1. **Chris Holbern:** Bikesharing works well in ______ areas. There are 114 ______ and 1,100 bikes. You can join for a year, a ______, or a day. Bikesharing is not only open to residents but ______ too.
2. **Matt Pearson:** The program is great for ______ and it brings more people to the ______ area.
3. **Chris:** The bike has ______ speeds, a basket, a bell, and a ______ for use at night.
4. **Matt:** The bikes are not only safe but ______ too.
5. **Chris:** We have to keep the system ______ and fix the bikes. When a station gets too full, we have a ______ that picks up bikes and transfers them to another ______.
6. **Matt:** Businesses think that bikeshare has improved their ______ ______.

C Read the sentences. Then listen to each speaker in the video and choose the correct answer.

1. 

2. 

3. 

4. 

5. 

______ a. Bikesharing helped me to lose weight.
______ b. I don't worry about anyone stealing my bike.
______ c. I use bikeshare day or night when I'm visiting Washington.
______ d. You can check ahead to see if any bikes are available.
______ e. A lot of professional people like me use bikeshare.

Ask Answer Would you use bikeshare? What are some of the disadvantages of a bikesharing program?

Connections

A Read the description of a bikesharing program in Exercise **A** on page 77. Would it work in your city or town? Why or why not?

B Read the facts about the bikesharing program. Then read about Henry's and Giovanni's opinions on bikesharing. Add one more item to each person's list.

Bikesharing program, FACTS

- Membership costs $90 a year.
- Helmets are not provided.
- Five hundred single-speed bikes are available.

Henry

I support bikesharing. I think we should introduce a bikesharing system in my city.

The bikesharing system . . .

— gives you an easy and reliable way to get around town.
— promotes sustainable transportation.
— is a good option when the subways are delayed.
— is easy to navigate—anyone can use it.
— saves you time between transfers.
— means you can avoid cramped subway cars.
— ________________.

Giovanni

I'm against bikesharing. I think we should lower the fares and encourage people to use the subway.

The bikesharing system . . .

— will take taxpayer money to maintain and take money away from other transportation projects.
— will overwhelm the streets with too many bikes.
— doesn't provide helmets for riders and therefore puts people's lives at risk.
— is not suitable for long-distance trips.
— is not affordable for some people.
— ________________________________.

C Do a role-play.

Student A: You agree with Henry. Explain why you support bikesharing. Compare it to riding the subway.

Student B: You agree with Giovanni. Explain why you are against bikesharing. Compare it to riding the subway.

Bikesharing is a good idea. For shorter distances, it's faster than waiting for a bus or the subway.

It may be faster in some cases, but it's not as safe. Keep in mind that bikesharing will put more bicyclists on the road. As a result . . .

Writing

A Letter of Complaint

A What would you do if bus and subway fares increased two times in one year?

☐ 1. Call or e-mail my complaint to the city.
☐ 2. Complain to my family and friends about how unfair it is.
☐ 3. Just accept it and do nothing.

B Read Joanna's letter of complaint. Then answer the questions with a partner.

Dear Representative Meyer,

Recently you voted against a bikesharing plan for our city. I'm writing to ask that you support it.

As a commuter on the Blue Line, I used to transfer from the subway to the B41 bus to get to my office. As you know, because of the weak economy, there have been transportation cuts. As a result, the B41 bus line has been eliminated, and I have no reliable way to get to work easily.

The distance between the subway station and my office is too far to walk. A cab is one option, but taking a taxi is expensive. I'm feeling very frustrated by this situation.

A bikesharing system would not only be good for the city (fewer people riding in cars means less pollution), but it's also convenient for someone like me: I need to travel between the subway and my office quickly and safely, and riding a bike would be the perfect solution for me!

Thank you for your attention to this matter,

Joanna O'Shea

TIP State your request up front. Present the problem. Show cause and effect where possible.

TIP Offer a solution and explain how it helps.

1. Who is the letter written to?
2. What's Joanna's problem?
3. What caused it?
4. What's her solution?

C Think of a problem you'd like to see changed. Choose from the problems below or use your own idea. On a separate piece of paper, write notes about the problem, its causes, and a solution.

If you live in a city, write about . . .

- the increasing cost of public transportation
- traffic congestion
- cuts in transportation services

If you live in a town, write about . . .

- the lack of a subway or bus system
- poor transportation options to nearby towns
- the lack of easy access to a major airport

D Write a letter of complaint using your notes. Be sure to use the writing tips. Then exchange papers with another student. Read your partner's letter. Does it do the three things on the Writing Checklist? Do you think the request will be granted? Why or why not?

Writing Checklist

Does the letter . . .

1. state the writer's request clearly?
2. explain what the problem is and what caused it?
3. offer a possible solution?

Reading

A Read the statistics below and then ask your partner: How does your country compare to the ones in the chart? Do many people from other nations come to live in your country permanently or temporarily? If so, where do they come from?

People all over the globe are on the move, with many moving permanently or temporarily to a country other than their own.

Country	% of the population that is foreign-born
Canada	18.7%
India	0.5%
Singapore	42.6%
Germany	12.3%

B Read the article. What is the main point of this article?

a. The parents and students disagree over cars and driving rules.
b. All students dream about getting away and going somewhere fun.
c. The student body is diverse, but they all share an interest in cars.
d. The students' diverse backgrounds help them to get a driver's license.

C Quickly find and underline the answers to questions 1–6 in the reading. Then take turns asking and answering them with a partner.

1. How old do the students need to be to get a license?
2. Why do they want a car?
3. Where do they want to go?
4. What kind of car do they want?
5. What kind of car do their parents want them to drive?
6. What are some of the rules they have to follow?

D Look at these ideas from the reading about driving. What do you think they mean? Which ones do you agree with?

1. "Your car is your life."
2. "Doesn't everyone want to get away?"
3. "The teens want a new car that makes a statement."

Ask Answer In the United States, a driver's first car symbolizes independence and adulthood. Does driving have the same meaning for you? What symbolizes independence in your culture?

ONE FOOT on the GAS

Everyone has a backpack. Boys tend to wear jeans and T-shirts; girls wear skirts or pants. Boys and girls wear earrings and talk about the same music. To an outsider, it looks like just another typical day at J.E.B. Stuart High School.

But running beneath the common fashion and attitude[1] are their cultural differences at home: many of the students have parents who came to the United States from other countries. Walking through the halls of Stuart, one meets students from a variety of different backgrounds: an African American, an Afghan Italian, a Cambodian, and a Palestinian. The students take pride in their diversity even as they try to fit in as everyday American teenagers.

Conversations, especially among the boys, quickly turn to cars. "A car means freedom," one says. "You can go anywhere—your car is your life." One boy, who is saving his part-time job earnings[2] for a car, says, "With a car I could go with my friends to the beach or to New York. Life in general can get overwhelming sometimes. Doesn't everyone want to get away?"

And get away they do. Teenagers in many states in the United States can get a license at the age of 16 and most are eager to start driving right away. Teen drivers have a higher rate of road accidents, however. Because of that, the student drivers at Stuart will have to follow their parents' rules: No talking or texting on your cell phone while driving. Remember to wear your seat belt. Don't drive too fast. Commuting to school is all right, but driving in the city's rush hour is not allowed. When taking the car out, remember to bring it home on time. Being safe, reliable, and punctual is important, say parents.

For most new drivers, it's important for a car to be attractive and cool: They want a new car that can "make a statement." Their parents, on the other hand, are looking for a car for their child that is economical, affordable, and most of all, safe. As a result, most teens start driving with the family car that's available—which is usually the oldest, least attractive one of the bunch.

Back at Stuart High, at 2:05 p.m., the school day ends, and a rush to buses and cars begins. Some students get rides with parents or friends. Others get to drive themselves. Music blares[3] from car radios and the kids who are left behind sit on the grass talking, laughing, and just hanging out with friends.

These are normal American teenagers whose parents happen to come from all over the world. They may have one foot in their parents' culture, but they share one thing with their US-born classmates: They all have one foot on the gas pedal . . . and they are ready to go!

[1] **attitude** the way you think and feel about something
[2] **earnings** the money you make while working
[3] **blare** to make a loud, unpleasant sound

Speaking

A Read this information about Amadou and his parents. Then discuss the questions with a partner.

- Amadou is a first-year college student studying urban planning and transportation. He's an excellent student.
- His parents are from the Republic of Mali. They came to your country with Amadou when he was 2 years old.

- His parents have been working in your country for years without the proper work visas.
- Three months ago, Amadou was stopped for speeding in his car and the police realized he didn't have the proper papers.
- The government wants to send Amadou and his parents back to Mali because they are in the country illegally.
- Amadou wants to stay in your country, finish his education, and get a job.
- Amadou hasn't lived in Mali since he was a baby and he doesn't speak the language.

In your opinion, what should happen? Should Amadou be allowed to stay?

B Get into a group of three people. Two students will be attorneys (one supporting Amadou's position, the other against it). The other student will be a judge. Follow the steps below:

1. **Attorneys for and against Amadou:** Read the arguments below. Together, add one or two more reasons to your list. Also think about how you will address the arguments the other attorney presents.

   Judges: Read the arguments below. Together, add one or two more reasons. Also think about how you will address the arguments the attorneys will present.

Why Amadou should stay	Why Amadou should go
1. Amadou only knows this country. If he has to leave now, he may miss the chance to finish his education and have a better life.	1. The law is clear. Amadou's family broke the law when they entered your country on tourist visas and stayed on. They must all leave.
2. Amadou and his parents have worked hard and have never been in trouble with the law.	2. If you allow Amadou to stay in your country, many other foreigners will try to do the same thing.
3. Amadou did nothing wrong. He was brought to your country as a baby.	3. The economy is doing poorly, and many people are unemployed. Amadou and his parents will take jobs away from legal residents.
4. Last year, the government gave special work permits to 200 undocumented foreigners.	4. ______________ 5. ______________
5. ______________ 6. ______________	

2. **Begin the role-play.** The attorneys will argue their case for or against Amadou. The judges will listen to each point and can ask questions at any time. Use the Speaking Strategy to help you.

3. **Make a decision.** At the end, the judges should review their notes, consider the attorneys' arguments, and make a decision about Amadou's future. They should then explain their ruling.

Speaking Strategy

Presenting facts When making an argument, it is important to support your position with facts and evidence.

Considering that/Given that Amadou's parents broke the law . . .
Keeping in mind (that) Amadou doesn't want to be separated . . .
If you think about it, Amadou only knows life in this country . . .

Announcing your decision To show that you are making a fair, informed decision, acknowledge that you have heard and understood all the facts presented.

When I look at all the options, it's clear that . . .
After weighing all the options / factors, I have decided . . .
After much consideration, . . .

Expanding Your Fluency

Read these statements. Then join a partner and follow the steps below.

Talk about . . .

- the worst commute you ever had
- the first time you drove a car / flew in a plane / took a train
- the longest distance you've ever traveled
- your favorite car and why you like it
- why you would or wouldn't like to join a bikeshare program
- the best way to get around your city or town
- the worst thing about owning a car

1. Flip a coin to decide who goes first (Student **A**). **A** picks a statement and talks about it for a minute without stopping.
2. **B** goes next and can choose any statement except for the one that **A** already talked about.
3. Take turns talking for a minute until all the statements have been chosen once.
4. Award one point when a person can talk successfully for one minute without stopping. The winner is the person with the most points at the end.

Check What You Know

Rank how well you can perform these outcomes on a scale of 1–5 (5 being the best).

________ make comparisons
________ recognize cause-and-effect relationships
________ make a complaint and propose a solution
________ use facts and evidence to defend a position

8 Think Twice

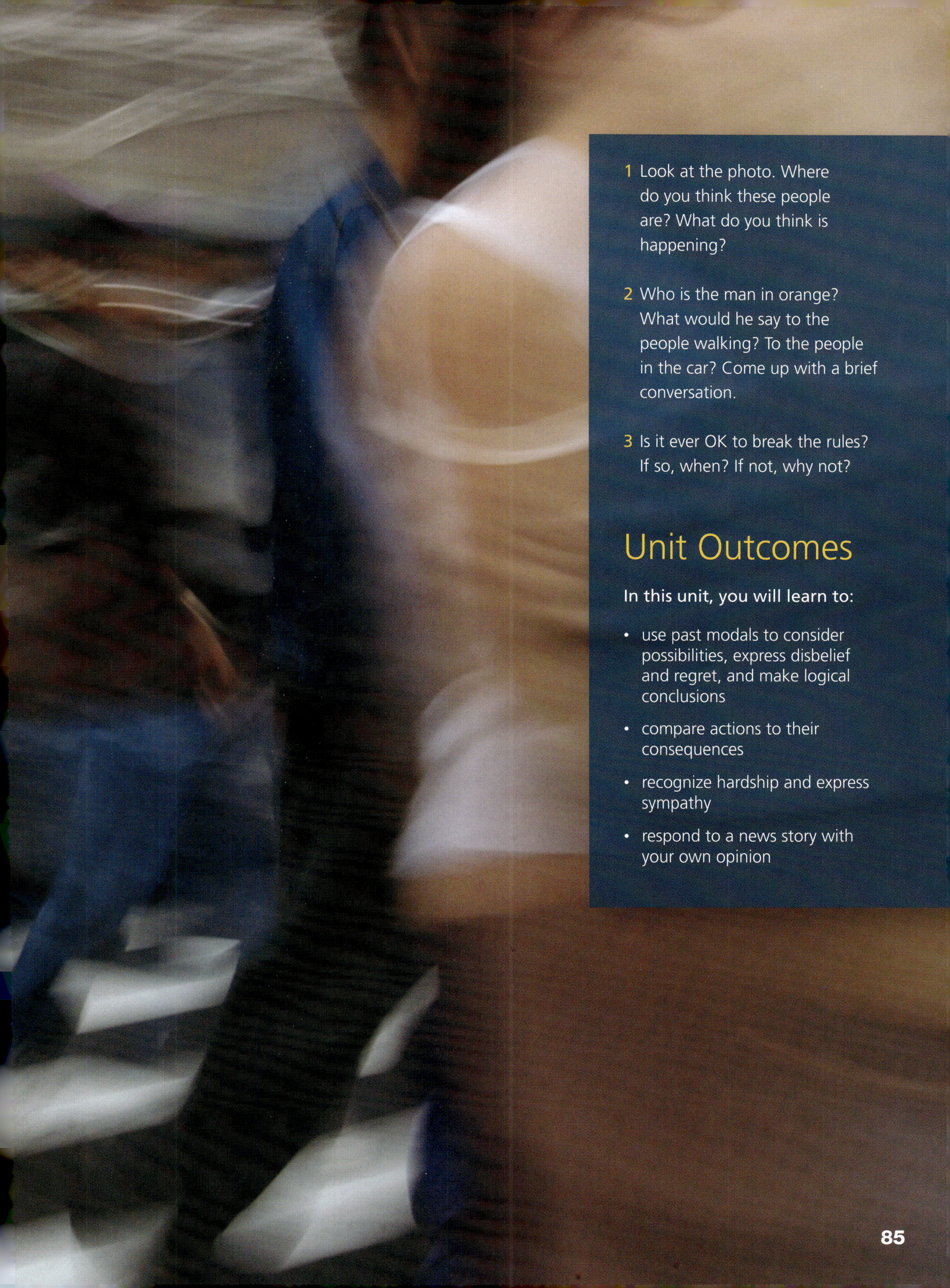

1 Look at the photo. Where do you think these people are? What do you think is happening?

2 Who is the man in orange? What would he say to the people walking? To the people in the car? Come up with a brief conversation.

3 Is it ever OK to break the rules? If so, when? If not, why not?

Unit Outcomes

In this unit, you will learn to:

- use past modals to consider possibilities, express disbelief and regret, and make logical conclusions
- compare actions to their consequences
- recognize hardship and express sympathy
- respond to a news story with your own opinion

Vocabulary

A Students often send text messages during class. Why do you think they do it? Discuss your answers with a partner.

consequences results or effects (of an action)
criticize to express disapproval by saying what's wrong with something
discipline self-control; an action taken to correct inappropriate behavior
disruptive causing trouble and stopping something from continuing as usual
get away with to do something wrong or risky and not suffer any consequences
get into trouble to be in a position where you will be punished for something
punish to take action against someone for inappropriate behavior
regulation an official rule (e.g., made by a government or school)
respectful to be polite and well-behaved towards someone (in authority)
restriction a limit on something

B Read these statements about texting in class. Who do you think said each one? Mark your answers and discuss with a partner. Which statements do you agree with? Why?

	Student	Teacher	Parent
1. I don't know of any restrictions on texting in class. It's not against the regulations, is it?			
2. I think there should be consequences for texting in class: for example, you should be punished in some way.			
3. It's a problem with discipline. Students who text in class are being disrespectful to their teachers and their classmates.			
4. All students would text during class if they weren't afraid of getting into trouble and being criticized by their classmates.			
5. Texting in class may be disruptive, but as long as they can get away with it some students will continue to do it.			

C Read the statements below. Answer the questions with a partner to discuss your opinions of these behaviors. Be prepared to share your thoughts with the class.

- talking in class without raising your hand
- looking at another student's work during a test
- coming to class without completing your homework

1. How are these behaviors disruptive? Which ones are serious discipline issues?
2. What are the consequences of these behaviors?
3. Which of these behaviors do people usually get away with?
4. What kinds of restrictions or regulations should be made to prevent these behaviors?

D In pairs, prepare a conversation where a student is caught texting in class by a very strict teacher. the teacher wants to punish him / her; the student asks for pardon. Use vocabulary from Exercise A.

Grammar

A Stella got in trouble for texting in class. Read the sentences in the chart to see what other students had to say about it. Then answer the questions.

Past Modals	
Use past modals with past participles to assess real or imaginary past actions.	
Disbelief / impossibility	Jen: Stella **couldn't have[1] been** texting. She lost her cell phone recently.
Possibility	Tom: She **might have[2] borrowed** a friend's phone to do it.
Logical conclusion	Amy: I heard she was texting her mother. It **must have been** something important.
Regret over an action that <u>wasn't</u> taken	Ed: Even so, she **should have waited** until after class to send a text.
Regret over an action that <u>was</u> taken	Min: I agree. She **shouldn't have disrupted** the class.
[1]or *can't have*	[2]or *could have* or *may have*

1. Who is certain that Stella needed to send a text in class?
2. Who is certain that Stella was *not* texting in class?
3. Who thinks that Stella made a mistake?
4. Who thinks it is possible that Stella was texting in class?

B Choose the correct answer to complete each item.

1. She loves scary rides. She **could have / must have** been excited to go on the roller coaster.
2. He **shouldn't have / can't have** been in the meeting. He was sick at home that day.
3. I'm not sure where Mike is. He **might have / should have** gone to the store.
4. We just needed one more goal and we **could have / couldn't have** won.
5. Our team is better. We **may have / should have** won the game.

C What happened? Read about these five situations. On a separate piece of paper, write 2–3 sentences for each one. Use past modals. Then take turns reading your sentences aloud with a partner.

1. You arrived at your friend's soccer game. You see your friend on the ground being helped by another player. Everyone looks worried.
2. Your coworker gets a phone call and looks surprised. She picks up her car keys and runs out of the office. She leaves her purse behind.
3. You've arrived at school and it's time to submit your homework. When you look in your backpack, it isn't there.
4. Earlier this afternoon, you saw your friend's parents talking to your homeroom teacher. Later you find out your friend has been punished for a month.
5. This morning, you saw your neighbor sitting on the back of an ambulance with a bandage on his head. His car is damaged on one side.

Connections

A Read the information about a contest. What are the rules of the contest? Would you ever enter a contest like this? Why or why not? Discuss with a partner.

THE CONCERT OF A LIFETIME!

Register at www.freeticket.cengage and win a free ticket to the upcoming rock concert by the Regulation Nation.
Restrictions: Must be 18+. Limit one entry per person.

B Now read about Mary's situation. Then discuss the questions with a partner.

Recently I entered a contest to win a free ticket to a concert featuring my favorite band, Regulation Nation. The contest regulations were clear: only one entry per name. To increase my chances of winning, I also entered the name of my best friend, Paola, without telling her.

My friend's name was chosen and she won the ticket to the concert. I expected her to give me the ticket because I was the one who signed up for the contest and she knows the band is my favorite. I was shocked when my friend said she was going to sell the ticket at full price.

When I refused to buy the ticket, she sold it to someone else. I missed the concert and I criticized Paola for what she did. Now we're not speaking.

1. What did Mary do? 2. How did Paola respond? 3. What happened in the end?

C Read these statements. Indicate if you agree with each one. Then explain your answers to a partner.

	Agree	Disagree
1. Paola must have needed the money.	☐	☐
2. Mary shouldn't have broken the rules in the first place.	☐	☐
3. Mary couldn't have known that Paola would sell the ticket.	☐	☐
4. Mary shouldn't have criticized Paola.	☐	☐
5. Paola and Mary must not have been very good friends after all.	☐	☐
6. Mary should have just accepted the consequences.	☐	☐

D What should Mary and Paola do now? Come up with a solution with your partner and act out a conversation where they repair their friendship.

Listening

big deal something important
get suspended temporarily not allowed to go to school or class because you've done something wrong
private only for one person or group; not for everyone
sympathetic showing that you understand and care about someone's suffering

A You are going to hear a conversation about student Micah Green. Read this excerpt from the conversation. What do you think Micah did? Discuss in pairs.

Carly: Did you hear what happened? Micah got suspended from school. For five days!
Mark: You're kidding!
Carly: No, I'm not. He got in trouble for posting something online.
Mark: What exactly did he do?

B What happened to Micah? Listen and complete the story.

Micah Green went online to (1) _______ a teacher. He deleted the post a (2) _______ later, but it was too (3) _______. The school (4) _______ Micah by suspending him. The principal said that Micah's posting was disruptive to (5) _______ life. Micah is going to write a letter of (6) _______ to the teacher he criticized.

Listening Strategy **Determining a Speaker's Attitude**
Some set expressions can give clues to a speaker's attitude or feelings. **Sympathy:** *I'm so sorry to hear that. / That's too bad. / I can't imagine what she's / he's going through.* **Surprise:** *No way! / You're kidding!* **Agreement:** *I know! / Tell me about it!*

C Listen again. In your notebook, write key words to answer each question. Write "NM" if the answer isn't mentioned.

1. What does Micah think of Mr. Salazar?
2. What is Mark's opinion of Mr. Salazar?
3. How did Mr. Salazar react?
4. How did Ms. Stevens describe the incident?
5. How do Mark and Carly feel about Micah's situation?
6. What do Mark and Carly think about posting opinions online?

PRONUNCIATION Notice how Mark pronounces *should have* as *should've* in the sentence. *He should've kept it private*. For more information on reduction with past modals, see page 150.

Writing

Give Your Opinion on an Event

invasion of privacy when your private life is disturbed in an unpleasant way
responsibility something that is your job or duty to deal with

A Read the short article about student Micah Green. What did he do and how was he punished for it? Discuss with a partner.

Student Micah Green was suspended from school for a week for criticizing one of his teachers online. Micah is the first student at the school to get into trouble for posting something on a social media site. Micah's parents will be meeting with the school's principal later this week.

B Read these online responses to Micah's situation. Which posting(s) do you agree with? Discuss with a partner.

soccermom As the parent of a child who goes to school with Micah, I'm upset. This is an invasion of privacy. Micah was at home and using his own computer. He was not at school nor was he using school property. I don't know of any school regulations that say you can't express your opinions about a teacher on your own time. Are there any?

celticsfan I go to Micah's school. As a student who spends a lot of time online myself, I can certainly sympathize with his situation. Does the punishment fit the behavior, though? Micah didn't use strong language and he took his post down after a short time. I think the school could have punished him in a different way—maybe by asking him to apologize to the teacher.

teacherman78 Being a teacher is hard work. We don't have very many behavior problems in my school, but there are some students who are disrespectful—just like Micah was. When an incident like this happens, you have to stop it right away. I think you need to make an example of the student. Was suspending Micah the right thing to do? I think so. Students need to take responsibility for their actions. What they do in and out of school has consequences.

C What do you think? Should Micah have been suspended? Write your own opinion to be posted online. Use the tips in the Writing Strategy.

D Exchange papers with another student. Read your partner's writing. Did your partner follow the tips in the Writing Strategy? Is your opinion similar to your partner's? How are your opinions different?

Writing Strategy — **Effective Online Posts**

When posting online . . .

1. Identify your role. *As the parent of a child . . . / I go to Micah's school.*
2. Explain how the issue relates to you. *As an Internet user myself . . . This is an invasion of privacy.*
3. Ask questions for further discussion. *Is that true? / Does the punishment fit the behavior?*
4. Try to summarize your ideas clearly or your audience may lose interest.
5. Remember to be respectful in your posting.

Video

goofy silly or ridiculous
illegal not allowed by law

reputation the opinion that people have about someone or something; how much they respect or admire it

reputation good / bad / solid ~; impact / harm / hurt / ruin one's ~; put one's ~ at risk

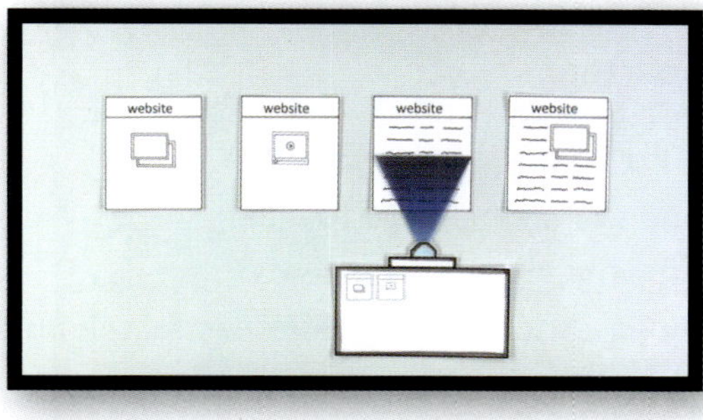

A You're going to watch a video about how to protect your reputation online. Discuss the questions with a partner.

1. What kind of information is available about you on the Web?
2. How could someone harm your reputation online?

B Watch the video. Mark each statement true or false.

	True	False
1. Search engines take pictures of everything posted on the Internet.	☐	☐
2. You don't have to worry about a problematic photo if the image is deleted.	☐	☐
3. It's easy to control who sees the photos you put online.	☐	☐
4. It's possible to hide your postings from search engines.	☐	☐

C Read this list of do's and dont's for posting online. Try to guess the missing words. Then watch the video and check your answers.

Do . . .	**Don't . . .**
think of the _________ who will see the posting (grandfather, boss, etc.)	share everything _________
take _________ for images, videos, and stories you share	use people's _________
ask your _________ to think about what they _________ on the Web	
_________ before you click	
_________ the person who posted a bad photo of you and ask them to ______ it	

Ask Answer Look back at your answers in Exercise **C**. Do you follow any of these suggestions already? In general, are you careful about protecting your reputation online?

Reading

anonymous made or done by a person whose name is not known

A Look at the photos and the title of the reading. What do you think is the main point of the article? Choose your answer and discuss your choice with a partner.

a. What we do in our private lives can show up online so there's a loss of privacy.
b. There are new ways to uncover a person's identity online so it's impossible to hide.
c. Anyone can post online so it's possible to get away with writing mean comments.
d. Two videos online show that there are negative consequences to behaving disrespectfully in public.

B Read the article and check your answer in Exercise **A**. Were you correct?

C Find the words and expressions in the article that are the opposite of the ones listed below.

Paragraph 1

1. Opposite of *identified* or *known:* ______________
2. Opposite of *leave alone:* ______________
3. Opposite of *public:* ______________

Paragraph 4

4. Opposite of *repaired:* ______________
5. Opposite of *posted (a video):* ______________

D Mark the statements that apply to the professional, the student, or both.

	The professional	The student
1. The person's behavior was caught on video.		
2. The video is online even now.		
3. The person damaged someone else's property.		
4. The person acted alone.		
5. The person knows that no laws were broken.		
6. The person said, "I'm sorry."		

E Summarize the professional's and student's stories using the chart in Exercise **D**. Then answer the questions with a partner.

- What were the consequences of their actions?
- Do you think video of them should have been posted online? Why or why not?

Ask Answer Imagine that everything you said and did today was posted online. How would you feel? How might you change your behavior?

Nowhere TO Hide

We used to view the Internet as a place of freedom—a world all its own. When you went on the Web, you could be yourself, take on a new identity and pretend to be someone else, or simply remain anonymous. Whatever you said or did stayed online and did not interfere with your life offline. Likewise, your private life was your own, completely separate from your online identity. You didn't have to worry about things you said or did at work or school showing up[1] on your computer. You could act goofy and it was no big deal.

Nowadays, new technology has changed everything, so that the separation between our two lives is no longer well-defined. What we do offline (in our "real" lives) can now be posted on the Web with a few easy clicks. With cheap cell phone cameras and free video hosting sites like YouTube readily available to anyone, photos and videos taken in public can be put online within minutes, sometimes with damaging results.

A professional in New York City discovered this the hard way. She was filmed on a commuter train on her way home, arguing with the train's conductor. "I lost control," the woman said. "I was very tired from a long day at work and I said some things I wish I hadn't." That short argument had negative consequences because the scene was filmed by another passenger on the train and posted online that evening. Thousands of people are still watching the video every month. "I was disrespectful, it's true," said the woman. "I didn't do anything illegal, but it feels like I did . . . because everyone is still criticizing me. It's been terrible."

A similar story happened in England when a young college student and his friends were filmed roughhousing[2] after a big football match. The young men damaged a car parked on the side of the road, and a video of the incident[3] was posted online and viewed by hundreds of thousands of people. "My friends and I apologized to the owner of the car and offered to pay him for the damages," said the student. "We felt so bad. But the video didn't show that. It only showed us damaging the car." The video was removed after a couple days, but the damage had been done. "I almost got suspended from school over this. My parents punished me. This experience has practically ruined my reputation."

We know that we're losing our anonymity online. And now, it seems we are losing privacy and anonymity offline as well. There are no restrictions around recording video of what happens in public and putting it on the Web. For now, you can get away with doing it.

It used to be a choice to go online and share yourself with the world. Now we are entering a time when someone else may be making that choice for us. In short, we may end up having a public face online—whether we like it or not.

[1] **showing up** appearing
[2] **roughhousing** fighting in a playful way
[3] **incident** an event

Speaking

surveillance the careful watching of someone, especially by the police

A We are under surveillance in different ways in our lives. Read about these situations in the boxes near each photo. What do you think about them?

B Discuss the three practices shown on this page and the questions below with a partner. Be prepared to share your opinions with the class.

- How do these different methods help us? How might they be an invasion of privacy?
- Which one do you think is most disruptive to our everyday life?
- What restrictions should be put on these different surveillance methods?
- Are you sympathetic to people who get into trouble in any of these situations? Why or why not?
- What should the punishment be if you get caught doing something illegal in each of these situations?

In the UK, there are more CCTVs (closed circuit televisions) per person than anywhere else in the world. They are used to track and photograph your every move.

Large numbers of people pass through airports every day. To keep everyone safe, new technology is being used to scan passengers who may be carrying dangerous items.

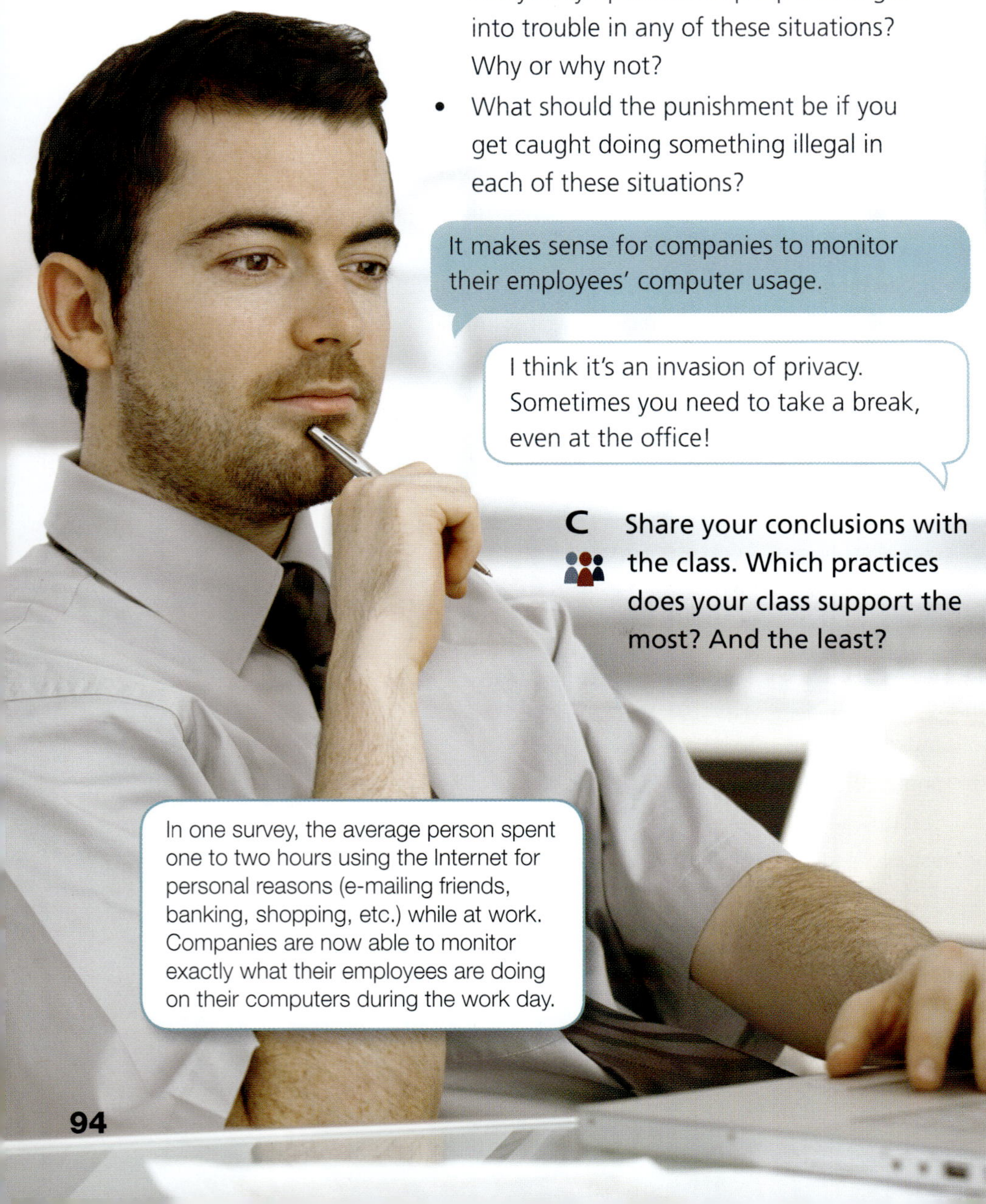

It makes sense for companies to monitor their employees' computer usage.

I think it's an invasion of privacy. Sometimes you need to take a break, even at the office!

C Share your conclusions with the class. Which practices does your class support the most? And the least?

In one survey, the average person spent one to two hours using the Internet for personal reasons (e-mailing friends, banking, shopping, etc.) while at work. Companies are now able to monitor exactly what their employees are doing on their computers during the work day.

Expanding Your Fluency

A Look at these two pictures. Where are these people? What do you think might happen in each case? Discuss with a partner.

B Now read about the laws shown in the photos in Exercise **A**.

1. Where I live, your ticket is not checked when you get on the metro. Sometimes, however, police officers make spot checks to see if all passengers have a ticket. Last month, my friend got caught on the train without a ticket. She was so embarrassed. She has to pay a fine of 40 euros.
2. If you smoke, you have to put your cigarette butt in the trash. It's illegal to litter. Last week, my coworker was in a hurry. There was no trash can nearby, so he threw his cigarette on the ground. Then he heard a police officer calling after him. This is the second time he's been caught for littering in a year. He may have to pay a large fine. He's very upset.

C Create a role-play about one of the situations in which you or your partner pretends to know the person involved.

Student A: Tell Student B about your friend or coworker. Explain what happened and how you feel about the situation.

Student B: Listen to the story. Ask questions to get more details. Tell how you feel about it.

My friend Hannah got in trouble on the metro.

What did she do?

She got on the train without a ticket.

Really? She shouldn't have done that!

I know, but she was in a hurry and . . .

Check What You Know

Rank how well you can perform these outcomes on a scale of 1–5 (5 being the best).

_________ use past modals to consider possibilities, express disbelief and regret, and make logical conclusions

_________ compare actions to their consequences

_________ recognize hardship and express sympathy

_________ respond to a news story with your own opinion

9 In the Wild

1 The animal in the photo is a macaque, or snow monkey, and is native to Japan. Is there an animal that is native to or often associated with your country?

2 In your opinion, can animals be intelligent? Which ones?

3 What story about animals was in the news recently? What happened?

Unit Outcomes

In this unit, you will learn to:

- use different forms of the passive voice
- use an outline to summarize ideas
- raise people's awareness about an issue
- write strong sentences to capture your readers' attention

Vocabulary

attack to try to hurt someone with physical violence
capture to catch a person or animal and confine it
cruel very mean or unkind
domesticated raised by people for agricultural purposes or living with people as household pets
endangered in danger of dying out completely
evolve to slowly change and develop over time into a different form
hunt to chase and kill an animal, usually for food
species a class of plants or animals that have the same characteristics
train to teach a person or animal how to do something
treat to behave in a certain way toward someone
wild free, untamed, not taken care of by people

Notice!
in the wild in nature

adv.	*treat (someone)* ***cruelly / fairly / poorly / well***
prep. + n.	*treat (someone)* ***with kindness / respect***
neg.	***mistreat*** to treat someone poorly

A Work with a partner to match an animal with a sentence. Then check your answers with the class.

Humans have been keeping animals as pets for thousands of years. How much do you know about three of the most common ones?

	Dog	Parrot	Cat
1. This is the most common household pet in the world.	☐	☐	☐
2. This was the first wild animal that humans domesticated.	☐	☐	☐
3. Not only can this animal sing, it can also be trained to talk!	☐	☐	☐
4. Ancient Egyptians treated this animal like a god.	☐	☐	☐
5. Many wild species of this animal are endangered.	☐	☐	☐
6. This animal evolved from the wolf and was originally used for hunting.	☐	☐	☐
7. Some people believe capturing this animal and keeping it in a cage is cruel.	☐	☐	☐
8. If this animal wags (moves) its tail from side to side, watch out. It's warning you that it might attack!	☐	☐	☐

A parrot

B Discuss the questions with a partner.

1. Do you, or does someone you know, have a pet? Is it trained to do anything?
2. What do you think of people who treat dogs like people (e.g., dressing them in clothes, feeding them at the table)?
3. Do you think it's cruel to hunt wild animals for sport? What about capturing and keeping them in zoos?
4. Name an endangered animal. Why is this animal at risk?

Grammar

A Complete the sentences in the chart with the passive form of sentences 2–6. Item 1 has been done as a model. Then check your answers with a partner.

1. People keep the animals in tiny cages.
2. Humans domesticated dogs 15,000 years ago.
3. Humans have trained them to do police and rescue work.
4. A volunteer is caring for the lost cat at the animal shelter.
5. The animal shelter will return the cat to its owner tomorrow.
6. Owners should keep their dogs on a leash.

Review of Passive Voice	
simple present	The animals **are** *kept* in tiny cages. It's cruel.
simple past	Dogs _______ ___________ 15,000 years ago.
present perfect	They _______ ___________ **trained** to do police and rescue work.
present continuous past continuous	The lost cat **is / was** ___________ **cared for** by a volunteer at the animal shelter.
simple future	The cat _______ **be** ___________ to its owner tomorrow.
with modals	Parrots **can** *be taught* to communicate with humans. Dogs **should** _______ ___________ on a leash.

❶ Forming the passive: Use a form of *be* + the past participle. With modals: modal + *be* + past participle
❷ To show who does the action, use *by* + noun: *The lost cat* **was found** *by a neighbor*.
If it's clear who does the action, or if it's not important, don't use *by* + noun: *Parrots* **can be taught** *to speak*.
❸ You might use the passive if:
- It's obvious who did something or the doer of the action is a general group of people: *Parrots can be taught to speak*. (We know humans are the ones teaching.)
- The action is more important than who does it: *The boy was bitten by a spider*.

B Complete the sentences using the passive form of the verb provided in parentheses.

1. Every year, thousands of cats and dogs (simple present: *abandon*) are abandoned by their owners.
2. Recently a celebrity wearing a fur coat (simple past: *attack*) ___________ by a group of animal activists. They say wearing fur is cruel. The celebrity says she (*should / allow*) ___________ to wear whatever she wants.
3. In the last forty years, almost 20% of the Amazon rain forest (present perfect: *cut down*) ___________ so that cattle (*can / raise*) ___________ there. Scientists fear that another 20% of the forest (simple future: *destroy*) ___________ by 2030.
4. A millionaire recently died, leaving all her money to her pet dog and nothing to her children. Now her wishes (present continuous: *challenge*) ___________ by the family. They say it is unfair that a dog (simple present: *treat*) ___________ better than a person.

C What should be done about the issues in Exercise **B**? Work with a partner to find at least one solution for each issue. Then share your ideas with another pair.

Every year, thousands of cats and dogs are abandoned by their owners.

I think the owners should be found and fined!

Listening

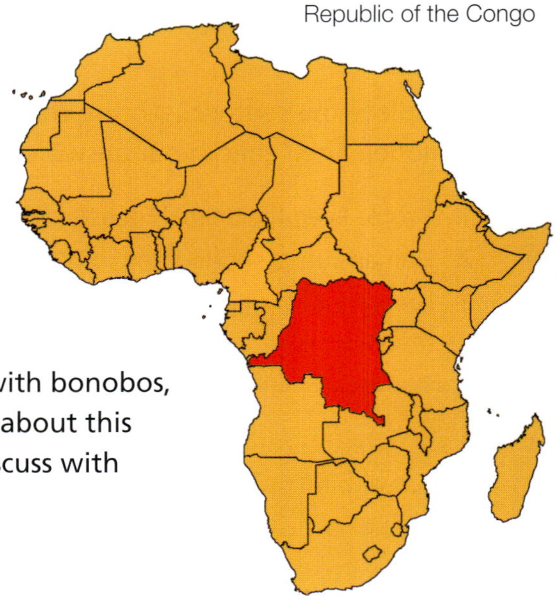

habitat the natural environment in which an animal or plant normally lives or grows
primate a type of mammal that includes humans, monkeys, and apes

A You are going to hear an interview with a man who works with bonobos, a type of ape. Look at the photo below. What do you know about this animal? Can you guess any of the answers to 1–4 below? Discuss with a partner.

Bonobo Fact Sheet

1. Country of origin in Africa: ______________________
2. How similar to humans: ____% of the same DNA
3. Behavior: ______________________
4. Endangered status: ______________________
   Reason: ______________________

Listening Strategy

Listening for probability
Listen for words and expressions like *possibly, probably, it's hard to say for sure, I think so, it hasn't been proven*. They are used to signal that a person is not 100% certain about something.

B Read the Listening Strategy. Then listen to the first part of the interview and do the following:

1. Complete items 1–4 above. Write only key words and numbers.
2. Then ask a partner: Which items are facts? Which are possible but haven't been proven? How do you know?

C Dr. Stern is going to describe a bonobo named Kanzi. Read the summary below. Then listen. Complete each blank with no more than three words.

Scientists are studying Kanzi because he's the first bonobo to learn to (1) ____________. The most surprising thing is that he wasn't (2) ____________ to use language. He learned it in the same way (3) ____________ do: he heard scientists talking to (4) ____________. Later, he tried to use words to (5) ____________ with people. Today, Kanzi can understand (6) ____________ of spoken words and communicates with people using a (7) ____________. He also plays (8) ____________!

D Discuss the questions with a partner.

1. How is Kanzi special? If you could ask him a question, what would it be?
2. Do you think capturing and studying animals like Kanzi is useful or cruel? Explain.

Name: Kanzi
Species: Bonobo
Home: Great Ape Trust (in the United States)

Connections

Mammoths were a relative of the elephant that became extinct about four thousand years ago.

clone a genetic copy of an animal that has been made in a lab using the DNA of another animal

A On your own, read the three situations. Come up with as many reasons *for* and *against* each situation as you can. List your ideas.

1. Ana is moving to another city and can't bring her dog with her. The pet needs a new home or it will be taken to an animal shelter. George has been thinking about getting a dog for some company and to encourage him to exercise more. However, he lives alone in a small apartment and tends to work long days, so the animal might be alone a lot. Should he take the dog?
2. Liz recently saw a movie that showed how animals are raised for food and she was shocked by how the animals were treated. Because of this, she's thinking about becoming a vegetarian. Should she?
3. Using cloning technology, scientists say that it is possible to bring back extinct animals, including those that died out recently (like some species of tiger) as well as those that became extinct thousands or millions of years ago (like mammoths or dinosaurs). Some of these animals would be kept in zoos; others would be released into the wild. Should scientists do it?

B Get into a group of four people. Follow the steps to discuss the situations in Exercise **A**.

1. Take ten small pieces of paper. Write "Yes" on five pieces and "No" on the other five. Shuffle the papers and place them face down.
2. Take nine small pieces of paper. Write the number 1 on three pieces. Do the same with the numbers 2 and 3. Shuffle the papers and place them face down next to the other pile.
3. One person starts. Turn over a paper from each pile.
    - 1, 2, or 3 is the situation you will speak about. *Yes* or *No* is the answer you will give to the question.
    - State your answer and give a reason to support it, using one of your *for* or *against* ideas from Exercise **A**. You cannot repeat a reason already given.
    - If your group members think you have given a good reason, you get a point. If you don't give a good reason or can't think of an answer, it's the next person's turn.
    - When you finish, return the papers to the bottom of each deck.
4. Play until everyone has answered as many questions as possible. Who has the most points?

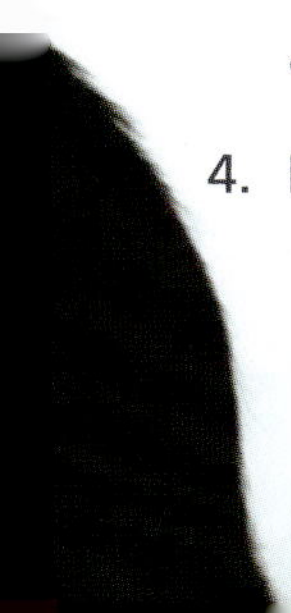

No, he shouldn't take the dog. It's cruel for a pet to be left alone all day in a small apartment. No animal should be treated like that.

Reading

A Cover the Quick Stats to the right and try to answer the questions with a partner. Then check your answers.

1. How many years do elephants usually live?
2. How long do male elephants stay with their mothers? How about female elephants?
3. Are elephants endangered?

Quick Stats: Elephants

1. Average life span in the wild: seventy years
2. Female elephants live in family groups called *herds*. Males stay with the herd until they are about 14; female relatives stay together for life.
3. Many are killed by poachers* for their ivory tusks and by farmers protecting their land. Some species are endangered.

***poacher** a person who illegally catches and kills an animal

B Read the title of the article, look at the photos, and read the outline below.

1. What do you think the Wildlife Trust in Kenya does?
2. Read the article to check your answer. Then complete the outline with information from the reading.

The David Sheldrick Wildlife Trust in Kenya

WHAT IT DOES

The Wildlife Trust raises orphan baby elephants until they are ____________________ to the wild.
To date, it has returned over ________ elephants to the wild.

HISTORY

The Wildlife Trust was started in 19___ by ________________.

HOW IT WORKS

Orphan babies arrive at the _________ in Nairobi.
Babies are cared for by ____________ who stay with them ________ a day.
When elephants are _____ years old, they are ____________________________.
Keepers reintroduce elephants to the ________ over _________________________.
Final goal: Elephants join ____.

THE BENEFITS

The work keeps elephant numbers from decreasing.
It maintains ____.

C What are some ways that humans and elephants are similar? Underline ideas that you find in the article. Did any of this information surprise you? Tell a partner.

D Using the outline, summarize for a partner what the David Sheldrick Wildlife Trust is doing in Kenya and why this work is important. In your opinion, what else can be done to help?

Orphan Elephants

Elephants, among the most intelligent creatures on Earth, may have no future without our help.

It's feeding time for the baby elephants at the David Sheldrick Wildlife Trust in Kenya. Here, orphan[1] elephants from all over the country are raised until they are strong enough to return to the wild. Most of them have lost their mothers and other family members to poachers or farmers protecting their land.

Moved[2] by the suffering of these animals, a woman named Daphne Sheldrick started a nursery[3] in Nairobi for orphan baby elephants in 1987. She named the project after her husband. Prior to this, she had cared for many of Kenya's native animals, but none interested—or challenged—her as much as the elephants. "Elephants are very human animals," says Sheldrick. "Their emotions are exactly the same as ours." In fact, studies now show that structures related to memory, self-awareness, and emotion in the elephant brain are very similar to those in humans. When young elephants arrive at the nursery, explains Sheldrick, "they've lost their families, and they come here filled with sadness and fear."

Enter the caregivers at the Nairobi nursery. With humans acting as their mothers, orphans are cared for by people called "keepers" who stay with them twenty-four hours a day. The other young elephants at the nursery help, too. Like humans, explains Sheldrick, "they are extremely social animals. Whenever we get a new baby here, the others will come around and lovingly put their trunks on its back to comfort it. They have such big hearts." When they are about 2, elephants are moved to a rehabilitation center in Tsavo National Park. Here, keepers slowly reintroduce the animals to the wild over several years, encouraging them to join one of the park's elephant families.

To date, Sheldrick's team has returned more than a hundred orphan elephants to the wild. The work being done not only helps to keep elephant numbers from decreasing; it has also helped to maintain the well-being of existing elephant populations. "The loss of older elephants," says one scientist, "and the extreme stress of seeing their family members killed, negatively influences a young elephant's normal development." When orphan females become adults, for example, they are less likely to care for the young properly. Male elephants become much more aggressive, which can also make them more of a danger to humans. When the young elephants are raised by stable[4] adults, however, these behaviors disappear.

Even after adult elephants have joined a new family in Tsavo National Park, some still come back to visit their human caretakers. In December 2008, Emily, a female that came to the Nairobi nursery in 1993, arrived at one of the rehabilitation centers one afternoon. "She'd given birth the day before, about a mile away," recalls one keeper. "She brought the baby here to show us her newborn." Even with a new life and family of her own, Emily—like other elephants—still remembered those at the Wildlife Trust who had loved and cared for her.

[1] **orphan** a child or animal whose parents are dead
[2] **moved** influenced emotionally
[3] **nursery** a place where the young are cared for
[4] **stable** calm, responsible

Video

VIDEO GLOSSARY

alert a warning, an alarm

anesthetic a drug that stops pain or causes you to fall asleep

collar (*noun*) an item that an animal wears around its neck; (*verb*) to capture an animal

GPS (global positioning system) a tool that allows you to locate or follow people or things on Earth

intercept to interrupt and stop something from happening

tag (*noun*) a device attached to someone or something that sounds an alarm; (*verb*) to put a tag on someone or something

A Work with a partner and do the following:

1. Explain what you already know about elephants. Why are so many of them being killed?
2. The title of the video is *Saving Elephants from Harm*. Watch the entire segment once through with the sound off. Then try to answer the questions.
   a. The people in the video are in Kenya. Who do you think they are?
   b. What exactly is being done to "help save elephants from harm"?

Did you know?

Elephants live in a group called a *herd*. The female lead in an elephant herd is called a *matriarch*. Everyone in the herd follows her.

B Read the paragraph below and try to predict some of the answers based on what you've seen. Then watch segment 1 of the video with the sound on and complete the summary. Finally, use it to answer questions 2a and 2b in Exercise **A** again with your partner.

Iain Douglas-Hamilton and David Daballen locate and then follow a herd. Iain is in an (1) __________ and David is on the (2) __________. When they identify the female to be (3) __________, they shoot her. The anesthetic drug causes her to fall down. Once she's unconscious, the team has only (4) __________ minutes to attach the (5) __________. It will allow the elephant to (6) __________ with Douglas-Hamilton by sending an (7) __________ to a cell phone via text message.

C Watch segment 2 of the video. Then match an item (1–4) with an action (a–d).

How geo-fencing works

1. An elephant
2. The GPS in the collar
3. The server
4. A person

a. gets it and stops a herd before it reaches a human settlement.
b. sends an alert to a list of recipients.
c. crosses a virtual fence line.
d. sends a text message (SMS) to a server in Nairobi.

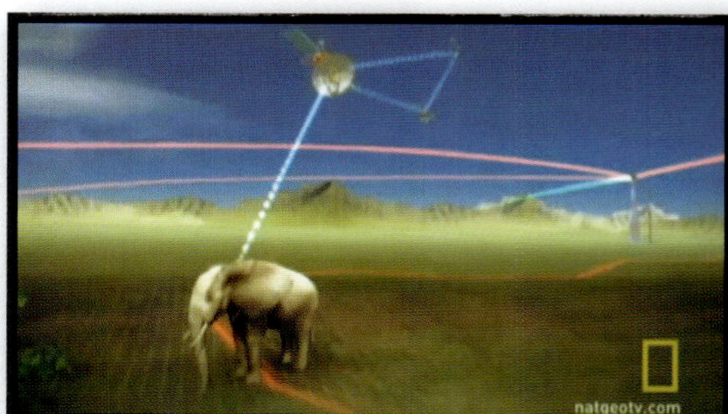

D Using the photo and your answers in Exercise **C**, explain to a partner how geo-fencing works. How does geo-fencing benefit the local people and help save elephants from harm?

Speaking

pesticides chemicals put on plants to kill insects

A Get into a group of three. Each person should choose one of the animals featured on this page. Then follow the steps.

1. **On your own**, read about your animal.
2. **Explain to your partners** in your own words the animal's current status and why people are concerned about this. Discuss what you think can be done about the problem.

Name: Siberian Tiger

Status: For years, tigers have been hunted for their fur and body parts (which are used in some cultures' traditional medicines). Their numbers have also been seriously reduced by the destruction of their forest habitat. Today, only 400–500 Siberian tigers—the world's largest cat—can be found in the wild.

Why the concern: Animal activists worry that the Siberian tiger may become extinct. In addition, because the tigers' habitat is being destroyed, it is harder for them to hunt. Though these tigers tend to avoid humans, they will attack and eat people if they can't find food.

Name: American Bumblebee

Status: According to a recent study, bumblebee numbers in the United States have dropped dramatically in the last twenty years. Some species have decreased by almost 96%. What's causing this? Climate change, pesticides, or something else—scientists aren't sure.

Why the concern: Domesticated bees are used to pollinate plants that give us many foods. Without the bees, less food will be produced, resulting in higher costs for consumers. Jobs are also at risk.

Name: Bottlenose Dolphin

Status: Though not listed as endangered, these animals are hunted worldwide for meat. Others are captured and sold for large amounts of money to aquariums around the world and used in animal shows.

Why the concern: Studies have shown that dolphins are not only playful, social animals, but that they are quite intelligent. Protesters argue that it is cruel to kill or cage an animal as smart as a dolphin.

B Imagine that you and your partners work for an international organization that will donate money to help one of the causes above. Which one would you give the money to? Why? Explain your reason to another group.

Writing

Create an Informational Brochure

World Animal Day
When: October 4
Why: to appreciate and learn about animals; to raise awareness of endangered animals

A A student created the brochure below to raise awareness about koalas for World Animal Day. Read the brochure. Then discuss the questions with a partner.

1. What kind of headline did the writer use? (See the Writing Strategy on the next page.)
2. Describe the image. Why do you think it was chosen? Do you like it?
3. Does the background information explain clearly why this animal is in trouble?
4. Which fact makes the strongest argument for helping the koala?
5. Is the call to action written clearly? What is one more thing you could do to help?
6. Overall, do you like the brochure? How would you improve it?

Use **an attention-grabbing sentence** that uses one of the writing strategies.

Use **images** that grab your readers' attention.

Include **a call to action** that tells people what to do.

This little guy might lose his home. Won't you help?

WHAT CAN YOU DO? Support or become a member of an organization like the World Wildlife Fund (WWF). Visit the site to learn more about how you can help.

BACKGROUND Though they can be seen in zoos all over the world, in the wild koalas can be found in only one place on Earth: the forests of Australia. For years, these unique animals were killed for sport and for their fur and almost became extinct. Fortunately, hunting koalas is now illegal. Protection programs have also introduced them into the wild again, which has helped their numbers to increase. Unfortunately, the koalas' natural habitat is still threatened as human populations expand into their forested land. Many koalas also die each year when they are hit by cars or are attacked by domesticated dogs that people keep as pets.

KOALA FACTS
- Although it looks like a cute little bear, the koala is actually a kind of animal called a marsupial. Female marsupials carry their babies in a pouch on their stomach.
- For the koala, the tree is life. They live and sleep in trees, they eat tree leaves, and they get most of their water from the leaves they eat. If the Australian forests disappear, so will the koalas.

B Work with a partner. You're going to create a brochure that raises people's awareness about an animal issue of your choice. Choose one of the animals in this unit or think of your own. Then design your brochure. Remember that it should have:

- an attention-grabbing headline.
- one or two compelling images.
- background information explaining what the issue is and two to four brief facts that will get people to care. You can use information you learned in this unit.
- a clear call to action that tells people what to do.

Writing Strategy

Getting a Reader's Attention When we write something—a brochure, a story, a news article—we want to get our readers interested in the subject matter immediately. One way to do this is to use an attention-grabbing headline or opening sentence. This might be . . .

- a question that makes you think: *Does having a pet make you healthier?*
- an interesting, surprising, or shocking fact: *In the last twenty years, 96% of these bees have vanished.*
- an emotional appeal: *Adopt a dog . . . save a life.*

C Exchange your brochure with another pair. Read their brochure and then answer questions 1–6 in Exercise **A** about it.

Expanding Your Fluency

Monkey freed from zoo by keeper, still hunted by police

Drowning surfer rescued by dolphins happy to be alive

Critics and supporters battle as bullfighting banned in Barcelona

A You are going to create a minute-long TV interview with a partner. Choose a news headline and, using it to help get you started, do the following:

Student A: You are the person from the news story (the zookeeper, the surfer, the critic or supporter of bullfighting). You're going to be interviewed by a TV news reporter about your experience. Work with your partner to invent a story. Think of answers to his / her questions that tell your story in a memorable way.

Student B: You're a TV news reporter. Think of five or six questions that you can ask your partner about his / her experience. If your interview is interesting enough, it will be shown around the world.

B Get together with another pair. Do your role-plays for each other. After you listen to the other pair's interview, answer the questions.

You say that while you were surfing, you were rescued by dolphins. What happened exactly?

- Who was being interviewed? What happened?
- Did the person tell an interesting story? Do you think the story will be shown around the world?

C Change roles and repeat Exercises **A** and **B**.

Check What You Know

Rank how well you can perform these outcomes on a scale of 1–5 (5 being the best).

________ use different forms of the passive voice
________ use an outline to summarize ideas
________ raise people's awareness about an issue
________ write strong sentences to capture your readers' attention

10 Decisions, Decisions

1 What does this image represent to you?

2 What was the last important decision you made? Did you make the right choice?

3 When you have to make a big decision, do you typically ask for help? If so, who do you ask and why? If not, why not?

Unit Outcomes

In this unit, you will learn to:

- use the conditional to make predictions and talk about hypothetical situations
- identify cause and effect relationships
- identify factors that influence decisions
- give reasons to justify a decision

Vocabulary

affect to influence or cause something to happen
change your mind to change your decision or opinion about something
concentrate to pay close attention to something
effect the result or change that one thing causes in a second thing
figure out to discover an answer or a solution to a problem
hesitate to not speak or act for a short time, usually because you are uncertain about something
process to review and consider information in order to understand it
rational logical, reasonable
react to respond or act in a certain way because of something that has happened
regret to feel very sorry about the outcome of something

A Look at the photos below. What are the people trying to do? Tell a partner.

B How much do you know about the brain and decision making? Complete each blank with a word from the word bank. Did any information surprise you? Tell a partner.

Word Partnership

Match each phrase with its definition:

keep (something) in mind	tell others honestly how you feel
make up your mind	remember
speak your mind	decide to do something

Did you know?

Your brain is able to (1) ______________ large amounts of information at speeds of 200 miles (322 km) per hour! That's faster than a supercomputer.

When we have too many choices, it can be difficult to (2) ______________ which *one* is best. In a situation like this, we often hesitate, change our mind many times, and then regret the choice we made!

A lack of sleep not only affects our ability to make (3) ______________ decisions; it also makes it hard to concentrate and (4)______________ quickly. People who don't get enough sleep have a big (5) ______________ on road safety, for example. Sleepy drivers cause over 100,000 car crashes a year!

C Complete the sentences with the words that describe you. Then explain your answers to a partner. Do you have anything in common?

1. When I have to make an important decision, I usually **react quickly and make a choice / take my time so I can make a rational decision / change my mind several times before I decide**.
2. I **often / sometimes / rarely** regret the decisions I make.
3. A lack of sleep **often / sometimes / rarely** affects my ability to concentrate in class.

Grammar

A Max is a college student who needs money for school. Read the advice he gets and then answer the questions with a partner.

Sam: You could get a part-time job in the evenings.

Max: Great idea. **If I do that, I'll have enough money.**

Jess: **If you had a scholarship, you would have enough money.**

Max: I know. I don't have a scholarship yet, but I'm planning on applying for one.

1. Look at the two **bolded** sentences. What does each describe: a possible future event or an imaginary situation? Write the sentences in the chart below.
2. What do you notice about the underlined verb forms?

The Conditional

❶ With possible (real) future events		❷ With imaginary (unreal) present situations	
if *clause*	*result clause*	if *clause*	*result clause*

❶ This form of the conditional is used to make predictions and talk about possible future events. The verb in the *if* clause is in the simple present. In the result clause, the verb is in the simple future.

❷ This form of the conditional is used to talk about imaginary present events. The information in the *if* clause is not true right now. The result clause describes an imagined result. The verb in the *if* clause is in the simple past. In the result clause, *would(n't)* + verb is used. Note: *be* → *were* for all subjects in the *if* clause: If I / you / he were the teacher . . .

B Complete the sentences with the correct word(s). Then explain your answers to a partner.

1. If the teacher is sick tomorrow, we **won't / wouldn't** have class.
2. We'll go to the beach this weekend if the weather **is / will be** nice.
3. I'm broke, but if I **have / had** a lot of money, I **will / would** start my own business.
4. I **will / would** travel to the year 2100 if I **have / had** a time machine.

C Complete each item with your own ideas and discuss your answers with a partner.

1. If you ____________________, you'll probably get a good job.
2. You'll score high on the TOEFL if you ____________________.
3. If you drink too much coffee before bed, you ____________________.
4. If you miss more than a week of this class, ____________________.
5. If I were ____________________, I would(n't) ____________________.
6. I ____________________ more often if I had the time.
7. I'd be happier if ____________________.

Listening

refund money you get back when you return something you've bought

return policy store rules about returning items that have been bought

A Listen to the conversations. After each, choose the best answer to the questions.

Conversation 1

1. The woman ____ a cooking class.
   a. regrets enrolling in
   b. wants to take
   c. has dropped

2. The man ____ the class.
   a. really enjoyed taking
   b. isn't familiar with
   c. has heard good things about

Conversation 2

3. Why does the man want to return the cell phone?
   a. There's something wrong with it.
   b. He's decided he doesn't want it.
   c. He's found a cheaper one somewhere else.

4. To get a full refund immediately, you must return the phone within ____ with ____.
   a. three weeks; the original packaging
   b. a month; a receipt
   c. two weeks; a receipt

5. Will the man be able to get a full refund in the store?
   a. Yes
   b. No
   c. It's not clear from the conversation.

Conversation 3

6. The man and woman ____.
   a. can't figure out when to meet
   b. are studying together from 4:30 to 6:30
   c. may or may not meet later today

7. When the woman suggests meeting at 4:30, the man hesitates because ____.
   a. he's made other plans
   b. he has class
   c. he wants to invite someone else

B Read the sentences below. Then listen again, paying attention to each speaker's intonation. Choose the best answer for each one.

1. **Conversation 1** The woman says *I can't wait* because she **is / isn't** looking forward to her class.
2. **Conversation 2** The man says *Oh, that's great* at the end, because he's **pleased / annoyed**.
3. **Conversation 3** When the man says *Uh, yeah . . . maybe* he means ***I'm not sure / Yes, I think so***.
4. **Conversation 3** The woman says *Oh, well . . . have fun* because she's **unhappy / happy** with the man's choice.

Ask Answer If you invited someone to do something (study together, see a movie) and the person said "maybe," would you expect the person to go with you?

Connections

hang out with the wrong crowd to spend time with bad people

A If a friend of yours started doing poorly in school, what would you do? Explain your choice to a partner.

a. I'd ask what was going on and give some advice—even if he/she didn't want it. I always speak my mind.
b. I'd talk to my friend, but I'd only give advice if I were asked for it.
c. I'd probably wait for my friend to talk to me. His / Her problems are none of my business.

Other: ______________________________

B Read the situation below with a partner. Then choose roles and create a role-play. Perform your role-plays for another pair.

STUDENT A You and your twin sibling (brother or sister) attend a very well-known and expensive private school. You each receive a scholarship to go there, but must maintain good grades to keep it. Your twin used to be a really good student, but recently started hanging out with the wrong crowd and studying less. His / Her grades are beginning to suffer. You can't figure out what to do, but you're worried that if your sibling doesn't concentrate on school, he / she will lose the scholarship. You're also worried your parents will be angry with *you* for not helping your sibling.

You want to find out what's wrong and persuade your twin to start doing better in school. Use the conditional to . . .

- make some predictions about what will happen if he/she doesn't make some changes.
- brainstorm some possible solutions to his/her problem.

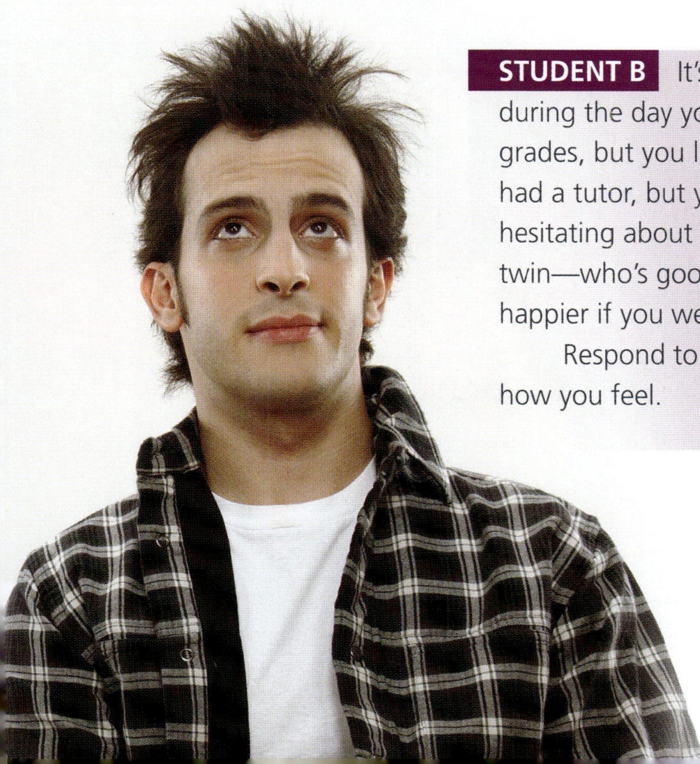

STUDENT B It's true: you're staying out late with your friends, and during the day you're having a hard time concentrating. It's affecting your grades, but you like hanging out with these people. It would help if you had a tutor, but you're not sure if your parents can afford one. You're also hesitating about asking for help because everyone compares you to your twin—who's good at everything. Sometimes you think maybe you'd be happier if you went to a different school.

Respond to your sibling's predictions and suggestions and explain how you feel.

If you stopped hanging out with those people, maybe you'd do better in school.

Yeah, but I'd also never have any fun. I'm tired of studying all the time.

Reading

A Read the title and subtitle and look at the photo. What do you think this reading is going to be about? Tell a partner.

B Read the article. Then answer the questions with a partner.

1. According to paragraph 1, what happens to us during our teenage years?
2. In paragraphs 2 and 3, the author describes two factors that increase our tendency to take risks during our teen years. What are they?
3. Does the author think these two behaviors are mostly good or bad? Why?

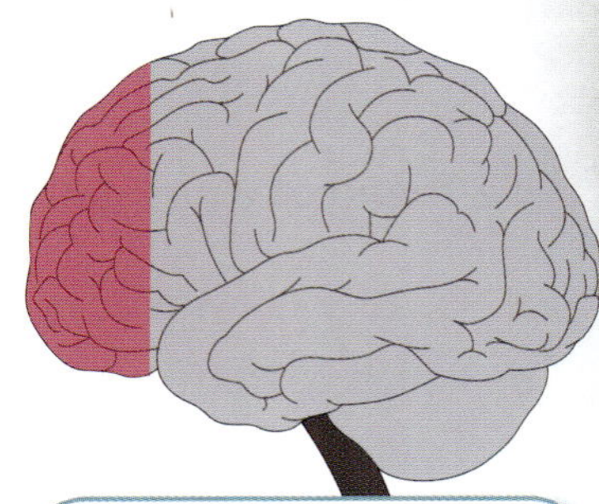

The prefrontal cortex—the part of the brain involved in making decisions, controlling our emotions, and planning for the future—isn't fully developed until we're 25.

C Choose the correct option for each item.

1. If something or someone is *maturing* (line 5), it is **developing / reducing**.
2. If you're *eager* (line 16) to do something, you really **hate / want** to do it.
3. Your *peer* (line 28) is someone who is **your own age / older than you**.
4. If you *impress* (line 43) someone, you cause the person to **dislike / admire** you.

ir- = not
What does *irrational* mean?

D Study the Reading Strategy. Then complete the cause / effect charts with information from the passage. Use no more than three words per blank.

Reading Strategy **Cause and Effect** In the article, the writer examines the cause / effect relationship between the brain and behavior. A cause / effect essay answers these questions: Why does something happen? What is the result of that event? As you read, think about these questions to help you identify key details.

Your brain produces chemicals.
↓
You want to try ______________ things.
↙ ↘
You meet ______________. → You're happier and ______________.
You drive ______________. → You get into a car accident.

A friend watches you play a video game.
↓
You want to get your peer's ______________.
↓
You ______________ red lights.
↓
You do well and get extra points.
↓
You ______________ your friend.

E Use the charts in Exercise **D** to answer the questions with a partner.

1. During our teen years, why are we so eager to experience new and exciting things? How can this benefit us? How can it be dangerous?
2. Peer approval is very important to us when we're teenagers. Why? How does the author use the video game to explain this?

Ask Answer How important is peer approval to you? Do you care a lot about what others think?

The Teenage Brain

Why do teenagers act the way they do? Science may have the answers.

For years, scientists believed that human brain development was completed by the time we were 10 or 11. Recent studies, however, show that during our teenage years, our brain—especially the prefrontal cortex—is still maturing in important ways. When we're teenagers, our decision-making ability is developing and we're learning to make good choices. At the same time, we're more likely than ever to take risks. Is this normal? Scientists who study the brain say "yes." In fact, they believe that risk-taking and other "irrational" behaviors may actually help teens to become successful adults.

Take, for example, the teenager's love of thrills. We all like new and exciting things, but never as much as we do during our teenage years. During this time of our lives, say scientists, our brains produce chemicals that make us very eager to experience new things—the more exciting, the better. Although the need for excitement can lead to dangerous behaviors (like driving a car too fast and getting into a car accident), it can also generate positive ones. The desire to meet new people, for instance, can help us make friends, which usually makes us happier and more successful in life. Taking risks and trying new things can be challenging or even dangerous, but this behavior can also lead to useful experiences that will benefit us as adults.

Psychologist Lawrence Steinberg created a video game to explore an important factor that affects typical teenage behavior: the intense need for peer approval.[1] In the game, players try to drive across a town as quickly as possible. Along the way there are several traffic lights. Some lights turn from green to yellow as you approach them. You must make a decision: should you slow down and prepare to stop when you see the yellow light or speed up and try to go through the light before it turns red? If you get through the light before it turns red, you get extra points. If you fail, you lose time and points. When teens played the game alone, they took as many chances as adults. When a friend came into the room to watch, though, the teen almost always tried to go through more red lights. Their goal: to get more points and impress their friend. Adults who took part in the experiment, however, drove no differently with a friend watching.

Why did the teens react this way and try to impress their friends? We enter a world made by our parents, say scientists. But we will live most of our lives and succeed (or not) in a world run by our peers. Therefore, it is important that we are accepted—and respected—by that group, even if it means taking some risks to fit in.

Anthropologists[2] have found that almost all of the world's cultures recognize the teenage years as a time during which people seek excitement, take more risks, and struggle for peer approval. Doing these things can help us become successful, independent adults. But, say scientists, we must also learn that our actions can have serious consequences and find a balance between the two.

[1] **approval** support or praise; respect
[2] **anthropologists** scientists who study people, societies, and culture

Speaking

A Read the definition of **peer pressure**. Have you ever felt pressured to go along with the group even when you didn't want to? Tell a partner.

> *If you do something because of **peer pressure**, you do it because other people in your social group are doing it.*

B Read each situation and think about your answers to the questions.

1. You have a close friend that your other friends don't like. You're having a party at your house this weekend. If you invite your good friend, your other friends will be angry with you. If you don't and your close friend finds out, he/she will be hurt. What would you do if . . .
   a. you were in this situation?
   b. you knew your close friend wouldn't find out about the party?
2. You're assigned to work on a group project with three other people in your English class. You have to agree on a topic. One person suggests an idea and everyone else seems to like it. What would you do if . . .
   a. you had a better idea?
   b. you were new in the school and the most popular person in your class suggested the original idea?
3. Your cousin is a compulsive shopper: the minute he gets money, he spends it. Recently, he lost his job and he's asked you for a loan. You have the money but don't want to loan it to him. What would you do if . . .
   a. your other relatives started pressuring you to change your mind?
   b. you found out that your cousin just bought himself a new cell phone and laptop?

C Take turns asking and answering the questions in Exercise **B** with a partner. Explain your reasons for your answers. What factors most influenced your decisions? At the end, rate yourself and your partner on how affected by peer pressure you each are. Do your ratings match?

Peer Pressure Ratings

- **Approval addict** Peer pressure affects you a lot; your decisions tend to be strongly influenced by the group. You need their approval!
- **The in-and-out crowd** Sometimes you're influenced by others' opinions, but you also have a mind of your own and don't always give in to peer pressure.
- **Independent forever** You're not affected at all by peer pressure. You think for yourself and speak your mind, whatever the consequences might be.

D With your partner, come up with your own question about peer pressure (like the ones in Exercise **B**). It can be about friends, family, school, or work. Then exchange your question with another pair. Answer the question you get.

Video

appropriate the correct thing to do
cognition a mental process used to think about things
inclination a feeling that makes you want to act in a certain way
intuition (*adj.* **intuitive**) a feeling that something is true even when you have no proof of it
plea an emotional request
rudimentary simple, basic

A Read the information below and then ask a partner: Who is Tyler and what kind of research project is he participating in?

At Princeton University in the United States, neuroscientists (people who study the brain) are doing research. They want to find answers to these questions: When we are faced with a dilemma (a difficult choice), how do we decide what to do? Which part(s) of the brain do we use to make our decision?

Tyler, the research subject, is put into a machine called a *scanner*. Tyler will look at some pictures and he will be asked some questions. The scanner will record his brain activity.

B Watch segment 1 and answer the questions. Check your answers with a partner.

1. What decision does Tyler have to make? Summarize it in two or three sentences.
2. What do you think Tyler is going to do?
3. If you were in this situation, what would you do? Why?

C Watch segment 2. Then mark the correct answers.

1. **The majority / very few** of the people who participated in this study **would / would not** help the woman.
2. When we're faced with a dilemma, there's increased activity in which part(s) of the brain? Mark your answer(s) on the image.
3. The findings from this study suggest that we're more likely to help _____.
   a. an attractive person than an unattractive one
   b. a woman in danger than a man in danger
   c. someone nearby than someone far away

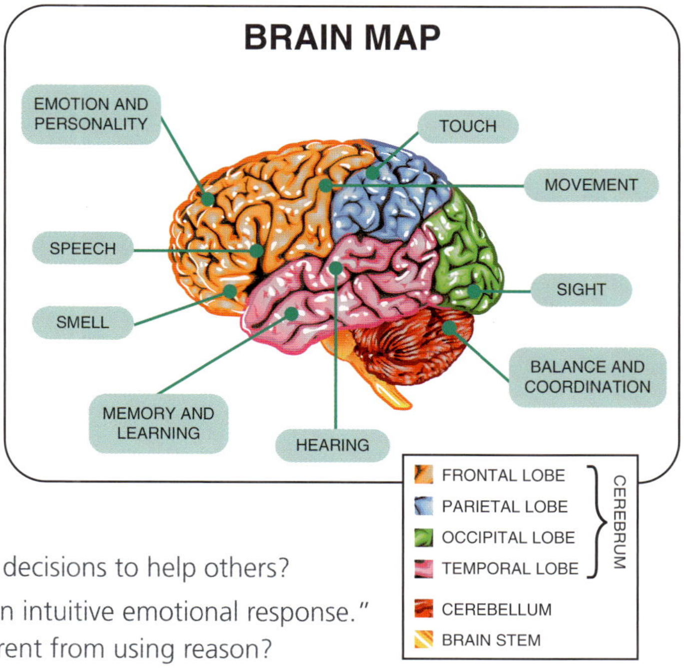

D Discuss the questions with a partner.

1. What does this study teach us about how we make decisions to help others?
2. Tyler's decision to help the woman was based on "an intuitive emotional response." How is using your intuition to make a decision different from using reason?
3. In what situations might you rely on your intuition to make a choice?
4. Do you think our intuition can help us make good decisions? Why or why not? Do you tend to rely more on your intuition, reason, or both when you make important choices? Why?

Writing

Showing Cause and Effect

A Read the scenario below and then one student's response to the question. What does he decide to do? What reasons does he give? Tell a partner.

You've been accepted to two universities. One is based in a small city near your hometown, where you're now living. Another is over 400 km away in a big city. Below is some information about the schools.

School near your hometown	School in the big city
• You'll live at home in your own room. • You'll be living in your hometown where everything is familiar. • All of your friends are going to this school, so you'll still see them all the time. • Classes will be small and you'll get lots of attention. • Your school will be a local college where you'll get a good education. • Tuition is affordable and you'll save money because you'll be living at home. • Your parents prefer this college.	• You'll live in a dorm with two roommates. • You'll be living in a big city that you've never been to before. • You won't know anyone, so you'll make new friends. • Classes will be very large. • Your school will be a prestigious school where you'll get a good education. • Tuition is affordable, but doesn't cover other school-related expenses. • Your teachers prefer this college.

Question: If you were in this situation, which school would you attend? Which factors would affect your decision the most?

Response: If I were in this situation, I'd probably go to the local school for two main reasons. First, it would be cheaper. When you go away to school, you typically eat in the dorm cafeteria, which costs extra. You also have a lot of living expenses that you don't have when you live at home. It can get expensive. If I went to a local school, I wouldn't have to pay to live in a dorm. I also wouldn't need to decorate my room. I'd save money on food, too, because I'd be eating my meals at home. **Consequently**, I'd be able to use my money for other things. Another reason I wouldn't move is that I would miss my friends and especially my family. I'm one of three children and we're all really close. If I moved, I'd only see my family during breaks. **As a result**, I'd probably be kind of lonely. If I went to the local school, though, I'd still see my friends and family all the time. **Because of this**, I'd probably be happier and do better in school. For these two reasons, I'd choose to go to the local school.

B Think about how you would answer the question in Exercise A. Then do the following:

1. On a separate piece of paper, list . . .
   - the school you'd go to.
   - two or three reasons for your choice.
   - what effects your choice would have.
2. Get together with a partner and explain your choice. Answer any questions your partner has and edit your notes.

C Using your notes, write a paragraph answering the question in Exercise **A**. As you write, remember to give two reasons for your choice. Also, explain what effects your choice would have. Use the information in the Writing Strategy to help you write about causes and effects.

D Exchange papers with a new partner. Does it follow the instructions in Exercise **C**?

> **Writing Strategy**
>
> **Showing Cause and Effect** Conditional statements show a cause / effect relationship. Words and phrases like *as a result, because of this, consequently*, and *so* also describe results.
>
> If I lived in the dorm, I'd probably eat out a lot. (Living in the dorm would cause me to eat out.) **As a result / Because of this / Consequently**, I'd spend a lot of money.

Expanding Your Fluency

A Get into a group of four. Come up with two "What if" questions together.

What would you do if *you could change one thing about yourself?*

B On your own: Take two small pieces of paper. On each, write a question and your reply **using the conditional (*if* clause in the past + *would*)**. Don't explain your answer, and don't write your name.

C Put your two slips of paper in the middle of the desk and mix them up with everyone else's answers. Then follow the steps.

1. One person should choose a paper from the pile. (If you get your own, choose another.) Read the question and the reply aloud. Try to guess who said it.
   - If your guess is *correct*, you get a point. You must ask the author one more question about his or her answer. Then remove the paper from the pile.
   - If your guess is *incorrect*, put the paper back in the pile.
2. Now it's another person's turn. Repeat step 1 until all of the questions have been answered. The winner is the person with the most points.

Check What You Know

Rank how well you can perform these outcomes on a scale of 1–5 (5 being the best).

_________ use the conditional to make predictions and talk about hypothetical situations

_________ identify cause and effect relationships

_________ identify factors that influence decisions

_________ give reasons to justify a decision

11 Rain or Shine

1 Look at the picture. What do you think the weather will be like in an hour?

2 Describe your perfect day. What's the weather like? What kind of weather is your least favorite?

3 Have there been any major storms in the news lately? Where? What happened exactly?

Unit Outcomes

In this unit, you will learn to:

- explain how weather affects your life
- make inferences based on information you have learned
- understand and use similes
- use phrasal verbs

Vocabulary

assess to judge or decide the quality or amount of something
consider to think about something carefully
cut off to disconnect
freezing very cold
frigid extremely cold
give up to part with; to let go of
intervene to become involved in a situation and try to change it
look after to keep someone healthy or safe
mild moderately warm
postpone to delay (an event)
recover to become well again
refuse to decline something
take off to depart
tolerate to accept something that you may not like

A Weather can impact our lives in many ways. What is one way it affects your daily life? Discuss with a partner.

B Look at the photos and captions. What do you think happened to Jerri Nielsen? What risks are involved in taking this type of job?

Jerri Nielsen
Jerri Nielsen is a physician who gave up her job to work in Antarctica as the medical doctor for the Amundsen-Scott staff.

C Read Jerri Nielsen's story. Choose the correct verb to complete the sentences.

When Jerri was given an opportunity to work on the South Pole, she was so excited that she couldn't (1) **recover / refuse** the offer. She arrived in Antarctica ready for an adventure and she loved her new job. Halfway through her time on the South Pole, Jerri was shocked to discover she had cancer. At that point, Jerri (2) **assessed / postponed** her situation. It was too cold for a plane to come and rescue her. Any attempt would have to be (3) **assessed / postponed** until the weather became more (4) **mild / frigid**. Jerri's employers (5) **considered / looked after** sending a plane to rescue Jerri, but they canceled the plan because it was too dangerous. That was when the military (6) **cut off / intervened** in the situation because they had a plane that could fly in the (7) **freezing / cut off** air for a short period of time. A plane flew overhead without landing and dropped equipment and medicine for Jerri. She took the medicine to treat herself for several months. At the same time, she (8) **looked after / gave up** her colleagues as the doctor. And she waited. . . . Months later, she was rescued. Upon her return, Jerri received treatment and (9) **assessed / recovered** from her cancer. She wrote a book about her experience called *Ice Bound*.

D With a partner, retell Jerri's story in your own words.

Ask Answer Would you ever give up everything to move far away for a job? Would you be able to tolerate living in a place like the South Pole, cut off from everyone else?

Amundsen-Scott South Pole Station, Antarctica
From February through October, the temperature stays around –60°C. It's too cold for flights to take off or land. During this time, the workers there are cut off from the outside world.

Grammar

Phrasal Verbs

A phrasal verb is a verb + preposition/particle. Some phrasal verbs are "separable;" the verb can be "separated" from the preposition/particle by an object (noun or a pronoun). Notice the placement of the pronoun in the separable verbs. Phrasal verbs have different meanings than the base verb on its own, as you will see in Activity **A**.

	With an object	Without an object
separable	She **gave up** her job. / She **gave** her job **up**. ~~She gave up it~~. / She **gave** it **up**. Other examples: *put off, size up, think over*	She **bounced back** (recovered) from her illness. The plane **took off** on a dangerous mission. Other examples: *die down, pick up, step in*
inseparable	She **looked after** her colleagues. The doctor **looked after** them. Other examples: *find out, put up with*	

Some phrasal verbs have three words. They are always inseparable: *How much longer do we have to* ***put up with*** *this rain?*
Every winter I ***come down with*** *a cold.*

Bangkok floods of 2011

A Tam lives in Bangkok. Read his e-mails to his friend Pierre in Canada. Match each phrasal verb in the reading with a verb in this list that has the same meaning.

_____ assess
_____ became less
_____ consider
_____ discovered; learned
_____ increasing
_____ intervene
_____ postpone
_____ recover
_____ tolerate

October 6 It took me forever to get to the airport, where I (1) **found out** my flight was canceled. The winds are (2) **picking up** and it looks like it's going to start raining again.
October 7 It rained all night. The winds (3) **died down** this morning, so I went out to (4) **size up** the situation. This is the worst flooding I have ever seen. I'll have to (5) **put off** my trip for a couple of days.
October 9 I haven't been able to write since Internet service has been cut off because of the storm. They're saying the military is planning to (6) **step in** to help people with the flooding. I can't (7) **put up with** drinking soda and eating noodles much longer. I wonder when Bangkok will be able to (8) **bounce back** from this storm.
October 10 I'm going to have to cancel my plans to visit you. Why don't you come and visit me in December? (9) **Think** it **over** and let me know your answer.

B Work with a partner. What do these weather expressions mean? Look up any you don't know. Then give an opinion or make predictions about these types of weather. Use phrasal verbs where you can.

torrential rain	a cold spell	scattered showers	pouring rain
boiling hot	a heat wave	snow flurries	heat stroke

I can't put up with boiling hot temperatures. I prefer pouring rain!

Listening

A Look at the expressions below. What do you think they mean? Working with a partner, take a guess.

To describe weather	To describe people
break through	chill out
come down	freeze up
hold off	storm out

TIP You might notice that many phrasal verbs have more than one meaning. *Pick up*, for example, can mean (1) *to increase* (without an object), (2) or *to lift* (with an object, as in *pick up a bag*), (3) *to physically obtain* (as in *pick up a newspaper from the store*), or (4) *to learn* (as in *picking up a new language*). Which meaning is used in Conversation 3?

B Listen to the four conversations. Choose the answer that completes each sentence.

Conversation 1

1. Jill went to a(n) ___ party.
   a. anniversary
   b. birthday
   c. retirement
2. There was a(n) ___.
   a. argument
   b. performance
   c. announcement

Conversation 2

3. Bill is worried that ___.
   a. people won't come
   b. he isn't prepared
   c. it will rain
4. Dan is ___.
   a. confident
   b. unsure
   c. unhelpful

Conversation 3

5. Carrie wants to meet her friend at ___.
   a. school
   b. Deena's house
   c. the theater
6. In the end, Carrie is ___.
   a. staying home
   b. going out
   c. going to Deena's house

Conversation 4

7. Andy wants to ___.
   a. be on the baseball team
   b. appear in the school play
   c. graduate early
8. Andy feels ___ about his chances.
   a. unclear
   b. negative
   c. positive

C Listen again. What do these words mean?

1. storm out (Conversation 1)
2. hold off (Conversation 2)
3. break through (Conversation 2)
4. come down (Conversation 3)
5. chill out (Conversation 3)
6. freeze up (Conversation 4)

Ask Answer Have you ever stormed out of a room? If so, what made you so upset? What do you and your friends do to chill out? Think of a time when you froze up and didn't know what to do. What was the situation? How did it end?

Connections

break down to stop working properly
call off to cancel

A Look at the photos and answer the questions. Work with a partner. Where do you think these images are from? What do you know about the weather surrounding events like the ones you see here?

dust storm

blizzard

hurricane

B Work with a different partner. You are going to role-play a telephone call, sitting back to back so that you can't see each other's faces. Follow the steps. Use phrasal verbs in the box in your conversation when you can.

break down	*call off*	*chill out*	*come down*	*cut off*	*die down*
hold off	*put off*	*put up with*	*size up*	*be snowed in*	*take off*

Student A

Choose one of the photos above. You are on vacation in that place. Something has happened and now you have to cancel or change your plans. Imagine you are calling home to your friend, Student B. You should tell your partner:

What's happened

What you plan to do next

Student B

Your friend, Student A, is away on vacation (but you're not sure where). Suddenly the phone rings. It's your friend, calling you while still on vacation! You should ask your partner:

Where he/she is

How the vacation is going

C Switch roles and repeat Exercise **B** using a different photo.

Student A: There's been a huge snowstorm.

Student B: Is your flight going to take off as scheduled?

Student A: I don't think so. The snow is really coming down.

Student B: What are you going to do?

Video

batter to hit something with strong force
coastline the boundary between land and sea
defend to protect something against attack
erosion the gradual removal of rock and dirt by the weather (wind, the sea, etc.)
shrink to become smaller

A Look at the word bank and the photo. Answer the questions with a partner.

1. What is the video going to be about?
2. What do you think is causing it to happen?

B Read these sentences from the video. What do the underlined expressions mean?

1. If we didn't defend, nature would <u>take its course</u> and we'll lose more land. *to take its course* = **develop naturally / change direction** and come to an end
2. The sea walls themselves are <u>in a sorry state</u>. *in a sorry state* = in **good / poor** condition
3. We simply can't continue <u>to paper over the cracks</u>. *to paper over the cracks* = to fix something that is damaged so that it works **temporarily / permanently**

C Watch the video. Complete the chart with key words.

1. The problem
   a. The _______ Sea is eroding the coastline.
   b. Great Britain is _______.
2. Why it's happening
   a. The country is gradually tilting: Scotland _______ and England _______.
   b. Sea levels are rising due to global _______.
3. What the government is doing
   a. The government is spending a lot of money to _______ the coastline.
   b. Most of the money is used for _______ new sea walls and _______ older ones.
4. What they're doing in Essex
   a. They are flooding the salt marshes to _______ the coast.
   b. They are not building more _______.

Ask Answer Do you know of other places in the world that are slowly disappearing? Why is it happening?

salt marsh

Speaking

A Get into groups of four. Each student should read one story and then follow the steps.

1. Take turns explaining your story to the group.
2. What did you find surprising about each story? Discuss with your group.

❶ OTTO THE OCTOPUS

The staff of the Berlin Zoo look after many exotic animals, but none as popular as Otto the Octopus. He has a special skill. His handlers believe that Otto can predict when the sea is going to rise. When he floats at the top of the tank, it means that the seawater will soon be going up and the waves will be rough. If he sits at the bottom, the opposite effect will occur—winds will die down and the seas will be calm. The zoo staff recently postponed a boat trip to a nearby island due to Otto's prediction of "bad weather."

❷ THE DISAPPEARING CITY

The capital city of Mauritania (a country in West Africa) is known for its mild weather and central location within the country. It's also slowly disappearing . . . sections are being buried under sand from the nearby desert. After assessing the situation, residents tried building fences and pouring gasoline on the dunes, but nothing has seemed to work. At this point, they are used to putting up with the sand, but worried that they are losing their city.

❸ THE DAY IT RAINED FISH

On February 8, 2008, a strange rain started to come down in Kerala, India. As the winds picked up, local villagers reported that small, moving objects were falling out of the sky during the storm. It didn't take long to discover that they were fish! Scientists have some theories but are not sure how this could happen. The people who experienced it will never forget "the day it rained fish."

❹ MAKING IT RAIN

Have you ever considered what it would be like to change the weather? In the summer of 2010, scientists in Abu Dhabi did just that. They used a special machine to create more than fifty rainstorms—some with strong winds, hail, and lightning—on days when there were clear skies and no forecast of rain. They plan to keep on using this technology in areas where there is little to no rainfall. Needless to say, local residents were completely confused.

B These stories might all seem unbelievable, but only one of them is false. Which one do you think it is? Discuss with your group. Give reasons for your answer.

C Present your choice to the class and explain your reasoning. Your instructor will give you the correct answer. How many groups guessed correctly?

Reading

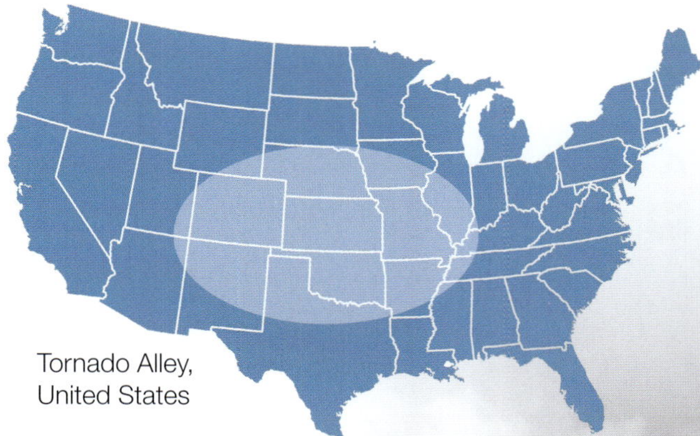

Tornado Alley, United States

A Look at the photo of a tornado and answer the questions. Discuss with a partner. Then read the article to check your answers.

1. What do you know about tornadoes?
2. Where and when do they occur most often?

B Read the article again. Cross out the one item from each list that doesn't belong. Then check your answers with a partner.

What the storm chasers measure	How long tornadoes can last	Where many tornadoes occur	Conditions necessary for tornadoes to occur
wind speed humidity temperature time of day	a whole day an hour or more a few seconds	flat ground crowded areas good places for farming central plains states	warm wet air cool dry air winds from the north

C What do these numbers refer to in the reading? Write your answers on a separate piece of paper.

about 1,000 | 40% | 48 kilometers (wide) | one in a thousand
one in five or six | F0 (winds of 64–116 kph) | F5 (winds starting at 419 kph)

D Read these inferences that are based on information in the article. Then explain why you think the inference is true, based on what you read.

> **Reading Strategy**
>
> **Making Inferences** An inference is a conclusion that you draw about something you read. You can guess something is true based on the information you have—even when it isn't stated directly in the article.
>
> Statement: *The tornado caused more than light damage.*
>
> Inference: *On the Fujita scale, the tornado was greater than an F0.*
>
> (This is probably true because an F0 tornado only causes light damage.)

1. Inference: The storm chasers are driving in a rural area. (paragraphs 1 and 3)

   This is probably true because . . .
2. Inference: No one has ever filmed the inside of a tornado. (paragraph 2)
3. Inference: Tornadoes are not easily formed. (paragraph 5)
4. Inference: The path of a tornado is unpredictable. (paragraph 9)

Ask Answer Tim Samaras has a dangerous job. What can you infer from the article about his personality? How similar are you to Tim? Would you ever do what he does? Why or why not?

STORM CHASERS

Two cars rush down a nearby dirt road straight at an approaching tornado. Storm chaser Tim Samaras, a 45-year-old electronics engineer from Denver, and his partner, Pat Porter, are in a van carrying equipment used to measure the tornado's wind speed and direction, air pressure, humidity (the amount of water in the air), and temperature.

Photographer Carsten Peter hangs halfway out the window of the other speeding car, which is driven by expert storm chaser Gene Rhoden. Carsten is excited. He wants to be the first person to film a tornado from the inside of the tornado itself.

The chasers can hear the tornado's jet engine roar and see it snapping power poles as they travel east past the local farms and directly into the path of the storm. It is not too far away, and the winds are picking up.

Tornadoes are among Earth's most violent natural acts. About a thousand of them happen in the United States each year, more than in any other country in the world. Some are weak and last only seconds, while others can cause damage for an hour or more.

Forty percent of all US tornadoes occur in the central plains states, agricultural[1] areas that are mostly flat. The "tornado season" occurs from March through July, when cool, dry air from the Rocky Mountains meets warm, wet air coming up from the Gulf of Mexico. In such open country you can see entire supercells (a rare kind of thunderstorm with especially strong winds), some as large as 48 kilometers wide. Only one in a thousand thunderstorms becomes a supercell, and only one in five or six supercells gives birth to a tornado.

Scientists measure tornadoes by the damage they cause. On the Fujita scale, named after Ted Fujita of the University of Chicago, an F0 storm does light damage with winds between 64 and 116 kph. The worst tornado, at level F5, does horrible damage with winds starting at 419 kph.

> "Storm chasers" are people who get close to violent storms in order to study and photograph them.

The clouds in the sky are spinning swiftly, and a confused bird flies in front of Gene Rhoden's car. And then a part of one cloud lowers and gathers into the shape of a funnel.[2] It spins like an angry ghost, no more than 3 kilometers from the storm chasers, looking like an alien[3] has come to Earth. The storm chasers are moving closer to the storm.

The tornado moves quickly through the fields, where it's destroying bushes and trees. Tim considers the situation carefully. He wants to find out all he can about the storm, but at the same time he must look after his team.

Before he can finish his assessment, the tornado does something strange. It seems to stand almost still, and then suddenly . . . it takes off, lifting up overhead. It's as if the sky were pulling a finger back into its fist. The winds have died down completely. The storm chasers pull their cars over to the side of the road to take a break. They've given up the chase for today.

[1] **agricultural** the science or practice of raising crops and animals (farming)
[2] **funnel** an object, which has a wide round opening at the top and a narrow tube at the bottom, used for pouring liquids
[3] **alien** a creature from another planet

Writing

A Vivid Description

A Discuss the questions with a partner.

1. How much does weather affect your daily life?
2. Why is there so much information (in newspapers, on TV, on the Internet) about the weather?

B Read Aleksei's essay about how a change in weather affected his daily life. What did you learn? Complete the first column about Aleksei's life in the chart below.

Where I live, we can have cold temperatures in the winter and gray skies with some snow. It doesn't typically get too cold, though, and it's usually sunny. That's why I was so surprised one week last February. We had a cold spell like no other. At one point, the temperature dropped down to –20°C. No matter how many layers of clothing I wore, I couldn't get warm. It was so frigid that we had to turn off the water because otherwise the pipes would freeze and burst.

To get to school on time, I had to get up early because I couldn't depend on the bus. Usually I take a short bus ride to get to school, but during the cold weather the bus was often late, so I had to walk to school. When I arrived, I felt so cold, like an ice cube. That put me in a bad mood. It was too cold to be outside for very long, so I stayed home every day after school. I got a little frustrated and bored. My little sister is cute, but she was always bothering me. She can be as annoying as a puppy—always running around and making noise.

When the weather finally became more mild, I didn't have to wear as many layers of clothing so it felt as if I had lost 10 kilos. I hope we don't have another cold spell like that again!

	Aleksei	**You**
1. typical weather		
2. change in the weather		
3. impact on getting around		
4. impact on home life		
5. impact on mood		

C Read the Writing Strategy. Then look back at the reading on page 129; use the strategy to complete the sentences below.

Imagine you were with Tim Samaras, chasing a tornado.

1. The weather was crazy, like ________________.
2. I felt as if ________________.
3. The wind was as strong as ________________.

Writing Strategy

Using Similes A simile is an expression that compares two things that the reader is familiar with in an unexpected way. We use similes (phrases with *like, as if*, and *as . . . as*) to make our writing more interesting and colorful for our readers.

When I arrived at school, I felt so cold, **like an ice cube**.

She can be **as annoying as a puppy**.

I didn't have to wear as many layers of clothing so it felt **as if I had lost 10 kilos**.

D Now write about a time when the weather affected your life. First, complete the second column in the chart in Exercise **B** with your information. Then, write your paragraphs. Use Aleksei's essay as an example. Include two or three comparisons using "like," "as if," and "as . . . as."

E Exchange papers with another student. Read your partner's writing. Does it clearly explain how weather affected daily life? Does it use similes to create a vivid image?

Expanding Your Fluency

A Some phrasal verbs have more than one meaning. Read about these three situations. What does "break down" mean in each case? Match each usage to its definition below.

1. You are driving in the country with your friend when your car **breaks down**. There is a thunderstorm approaching and you realize you've left your cell phone at home and your friend's phone isn't getting any reception.	2. You're studying in London and it's been a long and cold winter. You have a friend who is originally from the Caribbean who isn't used to cold weather. You see your friend at school and ask, "How are you?" Your friend **breaks down** and starts crying.	3. You borrowed money from a friend to repair your car windows after a storm. You recently got paid at work and were supposed to pay your friend back but you **broke down** and bought a new surfboard instead. What will you say to your friend?

a. to give in to something; lose control

b. to stop working properly

c. to get upset; become emotional

B Work with a partner. Choose one of the situations and create a minute-long role-play about it. In your dialog, you must also use three or four phrasal verbs that you learned in this unit.

C Get together with another pair and do your role-plays for each other. At the end of the other pair's role-play answer this question: How did they resolve the problem?

Check What You Know

Rank how well you can perform these outcomes on a scale of 1–5 (5 being the best).

________ explain how weather affects your life

________ make inferences based on information you have learned

________ understand and use similes

________ use phrasal verbs

12 What's Your Game?

1 What is this a picture of? Have you ever done this sport?

2 What do you prefer: watching sports or playing them?

3 List as many sports, games, and activities as you can. Circle the ones that are competitive. Underline the ones you do with a team. Which do you prefer and why?

Unit Outcomes

In this unit, you will learn to:

- use reported speech to explain what someone else said
- evaluate the relationship between activities and personal qualities
- pace yourself as you write a timed essay
- use an outline to support a presentation or essay

Vocabulary

achieve to succeed in doing something after a lot of effort
beat to win against someone and defeat them in a competition
championship a competition to find the best player or team in a particular sport
coach a person who trains others to play a sport
commitment dedication to doing something
defend to protect from harm or injury
get used to to become accustomed to something
in shape fit, healthy
motivation a strong desire or willingness to do something
obsessed constantly thinking about something
opponent a rival, especially in a game

A Look at the photos below and tell a partner anything you know about these sports.

B Read what Derek and Ana have to say about rugby and kickboxing, respectively. Complete each profile with a word from the list.

I'm a huge rugby fan. I grew up watching it with my dad and have been obsessed with the sport ever since. I played in university and now I'm the (1) ____________ of a high school rugby team that has won several national championships. People ask me how we've managed to (2) ____________ so many of our opponents. Part of it is talent and a team that works well together. But a big part is also each player's (3) ____________ to training hard and giving his best *every* day. It takes a lot of motivation and self-discipline, but that's what wins a game.

A friend told me that she was taking a kickboxing class and convinced me to join her. At first, every session was an intense workout, and I'd be exhausted by the end. After several classes, I got used to the exercises and started doing really well. Not only have I learned to (4) ____________ myself, now I'm (5) ____________ too, which has really increased my self-confidence. Studying kickboxing has taught me that you can (6) ____________ anything if you work hard enough.

Word Partnership

self- (combined with words in descriptions that relate to a person's own self). For example: *self-centered, self-conscious, self-defense, self-employed.* Find two more examples in Exercise **B**.

C Discuss the questions with a partner.

1. How did Derek and Ana get interested in their sports? What are the benefits of each one?
2. Which personal qualities do these sports help people develop? Add ideas to make a list.
    - Commitment to hard work
    - ____________________
    - ____________________
    - ____________________
3. How can these qualities help you succeed both on and off the playing field?

Grammar

Reported Speech

Use reported speech to explain what someone else has said. The verb tense, certain time words (such as *now, last week*), and pronouns can shift in reported speech.

Patterns in reported speech:

❶ verb + (*that*) clause: Ana **said (that) she was taking a kickboxing class.**
use with verbs: *explain, insist, mention, say*

❷ verb + pronoun/noun + (*that*) clause: Derek **told me (that) he played rugby.**
use with verbs: *convince, promise, remind, tell*

❸ verb + pronoun/noun + infinitive: Derek **encouraged his team to practice** more.
use with verbs: *beg, convince, encourage, invite, remind, tell*

Notice! Some verbs (*convince, remind, tell*) can follow more than one pattern.

Notice! Pattern 3 verbs are often used to ask for something or to give advice or instructions.

A Study the information in the chart. Then read sentences **a** and **b** below and do the following:

1. In sentence **b**, underline the pronouns and verbs that shift.
2. Which reported speech pattern (1, 2, or 3) does sentence **b** follow?
3. Use the verb *tell* and reported speech pattern 2 to report the sentences in **a**.

a. Direct speech: "I can't come tonight because I'm sick," said Al. "I think I ate some bad fish."
b. Reported speech: Al said he couldn't come tonight because he was sick. He thought he'd eaten some bad fish.

B Read the profile. With a partner, take turns reporting each statement about Marta's life.

When Marta was 14, a famous coach saw her playing soccer.

1. Coach → Marta's mother (*encourage*): "You should enroll Marta in a professional soccer camp."
   The coach encouraged Marta's mother to enroll Marta in a professional soccer camp.
2. Marta's mother (*explain*): "I don't have the money to do that."
3. Coach → Marta's mother (*promise*): "I'll take Marta to Rio and train her there."
4. Marta → her mother (*beg*): "Please let me go."

Marta's mother agreed. At 17, Marta was offered a spot on the Swedish women's soccer team Umea IK.

5. Coach → Marta (*convince*): "Take the job in Sweden."
6. Her opponents (*say*): "We've never seen anyone run that fast."

C Work with your class. One person says something about sports or games. The next person must repeat what that person said using reported speech and add something new. How long can you keep going?

I play chess.

Naomi said that she played chess. I've never played chess.

Naomi said that she played chess. Al said he'd never played chess. I like video games . . .

Marta Vieira da Silva
*Born in Brazil in 1986
*Soccer's greatest female player
*The female equivalent of soccer legends Pele and Ronaldo
*Is a Goodwill Ambassador for the UN

Listening

adjustment a change
handful a small amount of something
interpreter a person who translates what someone is saying into another language
NBA the professional basketball organization in North America
recruit to choose and try to persuade someone to work for your organization

A Professional athletes often play for teams in other countries. What challenges do you think they face when they move? Look at the profile of the basketball player below. What challenges do you think he might face? Discuss in pairs.

Name:	Jason Jennings (USA)
Age:	22
Years played a professional:	2
Country currently playing in:	China

B You're going to hear an interview with a professional basketball player. Listen and answer the questions below with key words and phrases. Then compare answers with a partner. Use reported speech to explain what the news announcers said.

1. Why is he famous?
2. Why is he in the news now?

The news announcer said that Jennings was . . .

C What challenges has Jason struggled with? Listen and mark your answers.

_____ 1. Difficult teammates and coaches
_____ 2. Missing familiar foods
_____ 3. Getting used to the weather
_____ 4. Making friends and socializing
_____ 5. Being the youngest on the team
_____ 6. A lack of privacy

D What did Jason say that made you choose your answers in Exercise **C**? Listen again and note the key phrases you hear on a piece of paper. Use reported speech to explain your answers to a partner.

He said that it was hard . . .

Olympic Stadium, Beijing

E Discuss the questions with a partner.

1. In general, how do you think Jason feels about his first overseas experience playing basketball? What did Jason say during the interview that makes you think this?
2. What is Jason planning to do next? Do you think his experience with his next team will be different?

Connections

physical education (PE) a school subject in which students exercise or play sports

role model someone you admire and try to imitate

violence an act that hurts, injures, or kills people

A Answer the questions in the chart. Then interview three people and take notes on their answers.

What's the best way to get in shape? Why?			
Me	**Partner 1**	**Partner 2**	**Partner 3**

B Get together with a new partner. Report your findings in Exercise **A** using four of the following verbs: *say, tell, suggest, insist, explain*. Which response do you agree with?

Carla explained that the best way to get in shape was to . . .

Notice! *Suggest* can be followed by a gerund or a *that clause*:
Carla suggested doing yoga to get in shape.
Carla suggested that the best way to get in shape was to do yoga.

C With your partner, do the following:

1. Choose one of the interview questions about sports below or come up with your own.
   - Do athletes make good role models?
   - Is there too much violence in professional sports?
   - Do professional athletes make too much money?
   - Should kids be required to take PE in school?
   - Should a person leave school before graduating to pursue a professional sports career?
   - Is the popularity of video gaming a problem?
   - Your idea: ______________________
2. Using the question you chose, interview three people each. You and your partner should not interview the same people. On a separate piece of paper, take notes on what each person tells you. Remember to ask people to explain their answers.
3. Share your answers with your partner using three of these verbs: *say, tell, suggest, insist, explain*. Then evaluate all six responses. Which answer was the most common? Which was the most convincing?

D Summarize your findings. Then share them with another pair.

We asked, "Do athletes make good role models? Most people said . . ., but one person had a different opinion. He suggested . . .

Reading

A **You are going to read an article about a Chinese martial art called *kung fu*. Look at the photos and then tell a partner anything you know about it.**

B **What is the connection of the items below to kung fu? Scan paragraphs 1 and 2 and write your answers on a separate piece of paper. Then check your answers with a partner.**

1. the Shaolin Temple in China the birthplace of kung fu
2. the fifth century
3. self-defense and battle
4. the city of Dengfeng
5. movie star, famous kickboxer, police or military officer

C **Read paragraphs 3 and 4. As you read, think about the questions below. When you are done, answer the questions with a partner using your own words.**

1. Who is Hu Zhengsheng? As a boy, why did he become interested in kung fu? How have his beliefs about it changed?
2. Think about the title of the article. According to Hu, what two sides are "battling for the soul of kung fu"? In his opinion, which one is winning?

D **Choose the correct word(s) to complete each sentence.**

1. *Adversity* (line 31) is a very **easy / difficult** situation.
2. A person with *character* (line 33) **is / isn't** able to deal effectively with difficult situations.
3. If you *get revenge* (line 37), you try to **understand / hurt** someone who has hurt you.
4. If a person *shows off* (line 51), he does things to **get attention / hide** from others.

E **Read the statements. Circle T (for *true*) if you think Hu would agree and F (for *false*) if he would not agree. Underline the information in the article that helped you choose your answers. Then explain your answers to a partner.**

1. A kung fu teacher's main goal is to show students how to fight well. **T F**
2. Kung fu films today are too violent and don't focus on the important things. **T F**
3. A kung fu master knows many different moves and why each is important. **T F**
4. The higher a student's kick or jump, the better at kung fu he or she is. **T F**
5. A lot of people today are studying kung fu for the wrong reasons. **T F**

Ask / Answer

Master Yang told Hu that "pride defeats man." What did he mean by this? How can learning this lesson help one practice kung fu more successfully? How can this advice help a person in life?

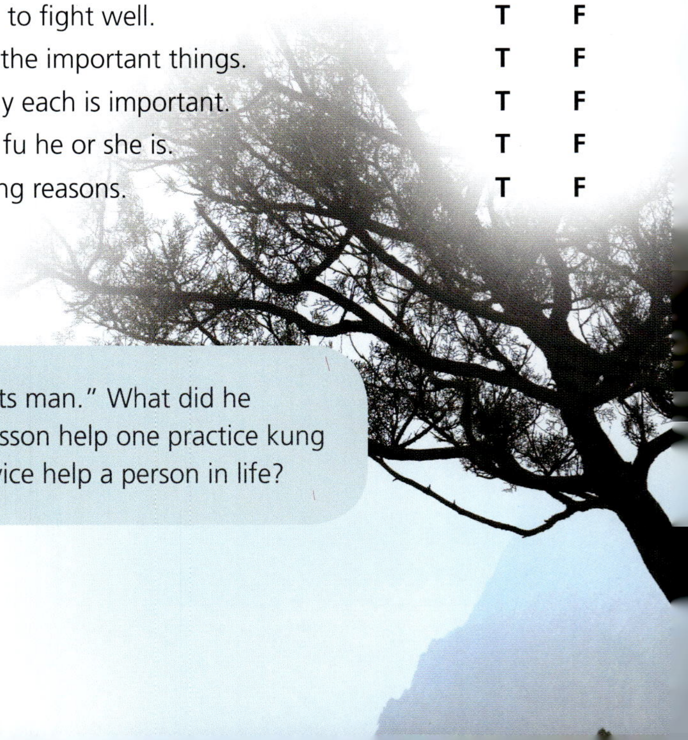

A Battle[1] for the Soul[2] of Kung Fu

The Shaolin temple in China.

Every year, thousands of tourists from all over the world visit the Shaolin Temple in China to see the birthplace of kung fu. It is here, says one popular story, that in the fifth century, a teacher from India taught a series of exercises to the monks at the temple. The monks adapted these moves for self-defense and over the next fourteen centuries used them in numerous battles.

Today, the Shaolin Temple is just a few kilometers from the city of Dengfeng, China's modern-day kung fu capital. In Dengfeng there are almost sixty martial arts academies with more than 50,000 students. These schools are attended by boys and girls from all over the country and every social class, ranging in age from 5 to their late 20s. Some arrive hoping to become movie stars or famous kickboxers. Others are motivated to learn skills that will get them good jobs in the military or police. A few are sent by their parents to learn discipline and hard work.

****

Hu Zhengsheng owns and runs a small school outside Dengfeng. At age 33, Hu has a handsome face and projects a confidence won through years of physical and mental testing. Unlike the big kung fu academies, which focus on acrobatics[3] and kickboxing, Hu teaches his 200 students the traditional Shaolin kung fu forms that his teacher, Yang Guiwu, passed on to him. Fighting is not the most important lesson of kung fu, Hu explains. He doesn't agree with how kung fu is often shown in the movies—a celebration of violence that ignores the more important teachings of respect for one's opponent. Instead, in his classes, Hu focuses on respect and responsibility. In each of his students he looks for a willingness to welcome adversity—getting up before sunrise, practicing in the rain—using it to control themselves and build character.

A Buddhist monk practices kung fu.

From his own experience Hu knows that one's idea of kung fu can change as a person matures. When he was young, he was obsessed with kung fu films and dreamed of using the moves to get revenge on bullies[4] in his village. At age 11 he entered the Shaolin Temple and was later introduced to his teacher Yang Guiwu. "When I met my master, I already had memorized many traditional moves," Hu says, "but he taught me the theory behind them—not just *how* to do something a certain way but *why*: He explained why I must move my arm a certain way. Why my weight must be on a certain part of my foot." Hu stands up to demonstrate. A strike[5] with your hand, he explains, is like a chess move. You hit the other person, but you are also prepared for how he will respond. Hu pauses. "Shaolin kung fu was not designed to entertain audiences or to attack schoolyard bullies." There are no high kicks or jumps, he explains. A kung fu master doesn't show off. Pride[6] defeats man and makes him weak, teacher Yang had told Hu as a boy. "It is hard for me to convince my students of this, though," he sighs. Today everyone studies kung fu to achieve something. Hu worries that the real meaning of studying this martial art, to learn about oneself, is being lost.

[1] **battle** a violent fight
[2] **soul** the spirit or most important part of something
[3] **acrobatics** difficult physical acts such as jumping high and balancing
[4] **bully** someone who uses their strength or power to hurt or scare others
[5] **strike** a hard hit using your hand
[6] **pride** a feeling that you are better or more important than others

Video

ascent a climb
ledge a narrow stand outside a window where you can put things

A Alain Robert is often called "the French 'Spiderman'." Look at the photos and watch the video once with the *sound off*. Then discuss the questions with a partner.

- What does Alain Robert do? How does he do it? Why do you think he does it?

B Read the statements. Then watch the video again with the *sound on* and mark the true statements. When you're done, correct the false ones so that they are true.

Alain Robert . . .	**True**	**False**
1. has climbed twenty buildings around the world.	☐	☐
2. normally uses no special equipment during a climb.	☐	☐
3. has never been arrested.	☐	☐
4. broke a world record.	☐	☐
5. has never rock climbed.	☐	☐
6. believes that climbing each building is a type of special test.	☐	☐

Alain Roberts climbing Tower One at Suntec City, Singapore.

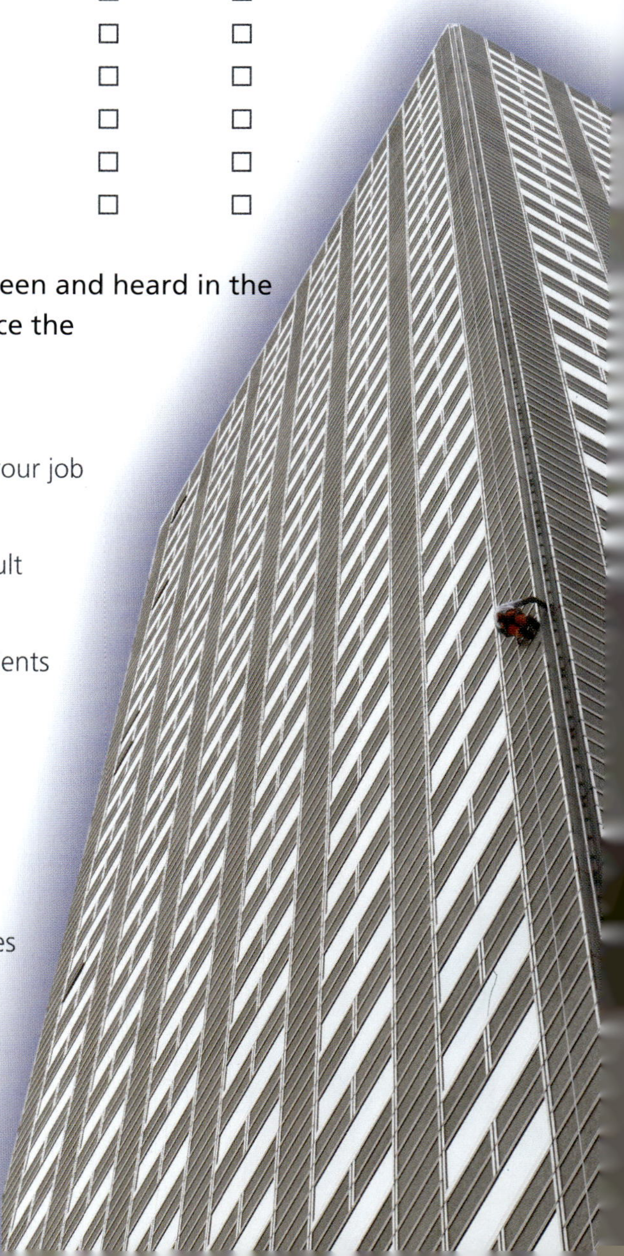

C Read sentences 1–4 below and think about what you've seen and heard in the video already. Then choose the synonym that could replace the underlined word in each sentence.

1. Would you <u>risk your life</u> for a sport?
   a. pay money b. put yourself in danger c. quit your job
2. As he climbs, one wrong move could be <u>fatal</u>.
   a. deadly b. uncertain c. difficult
3. Most people use <u>safety precautions</u>.
   a. insurance policies b. special equipment to prevent accidents
   c. official permits
4. His goal is to <u>overcome</u> his fear.
   a. understand b. ignore c. beat

D Get together with a partner and explain . . .

- in detail who Alain Robert is, how he climbs, and why he does it. Use your own words.
- how you feel about Alain Robert. Do you admire him? Why or why not?

Writing

Explain Important Qualities

A Think about the people you learned about in this unit. What are the three most important qualities necessary to be good at kung fu? How about for an urban climber like Alain Robert? Select ideas from the list and then explain them to a partner.

commitment to hard work	modesty	responsibility	strategy
courage	patience	self-confidence	strength
determination	quick thinking	self-discipline	your idea: ______

B Read the short essay below by a student about her experience on a debate team. What does it take to be good at this activity? Complete the chart and then check your answers with a partner. You will complete a writing task on the next page.

What it takes to be a good debater		
What you have to do	**Reason**	**Qualities needed**
prepare by doing research	*so you can debate the issue from all sides*	*commitment to hard work*

Notice the words in bold. The writer uses these to introduce and transition from one idea to the next.

The most important thing a good debater can do is prepare. Every debate focuses on a particular issue. In one debate I was in recently, we argued the pros and cons of playing video games. Whatever the issue, you must be ready to discuss it from your point of view and to respond to challenges from your opponents. Good debaters research the issue and study for hours before the debate so that they are ready. It's a lot of work and takes real commitment, but if you want to win you have to do it.

A good debater should also be able to speak persuasively. In addition to researching the issue, you must also be able to present and defend your ideas confidently and in a convincing way. This will score points for your team. Getting used to doing this in front of an audience takes a lot of practice—and courage. Good debaters are constantly working to perfect this skill.

Finally, a good debater stays focused even when things are difficult. During a debate, an opponent might say something unexpected or ask some hard questions. Some people get nervous when this happens, and this can cause a team to lose points. A good debater, though, stays calm and can think fast. Like speaking persuasively, this takes a lot of practice.

C Read the Writing Strategy. Then do the following:

1. Think of an activity that you enjoy now or played in the past. What do you have to do to be good at it? Why? Outline two or three ideas. Use the chart in Exercise **B** as a model.
2. Use your outline to write your short essay. You will have forty-five minutes to do this. Remember to save five minutes at the end to review your work.

Writing Strategy

Pacing Yourself On many standardized English exams, test takers are often asked to write a timed essay in which they must give an opinion. Assuming that you have twenty-five minutes total, remember to pace yourself and allow time for . . .

- organizing and outlining your essay (about five minutes)
- writing the essay (about thirty-five minutes)
- checking your work (about five minutes)

D When time is up, exchange papers with a partner. Read your partner's writing and answer the questions in the Writing Checklist.

Writing Checklist

Does the essay . . .

- identify the activity clearly?
- explain what you have to do to be good at it?
- identify which qualities are necessary?

Speaking

A In the writing activity, you created an outline that described what you have to do to be good at an activity. You are going to use that outline to give a short (one- or two-minute) presentation. Do the following:

1. Read the Speaking Strategy.
2. Review your outline and, on your own, practice giving your presentation a few times.

Speaking Strategy

Speaking from an Outline

Getting Started: Preview the Topic *I'm on the debate team at my school, and today I'd like to talk about what it takes to be a good debater.*

During the Presentation

Use transition words (like those in the essay on page 141) to help your audience follow you.

Do not just read from your outline; remember to look up at your audience periodically.

Try not to speak too fast, but be sure to pace yourself: you have two minutes total.

Closing: Summarize and Take Questions

So, in conclusion, I think you have to do three important things to be a good debater. . . .

Thanks for your attention. Any questions?

B Get into a group of three or four people and do the following:

1. One person should give his or her presentation. It should last one or two minutes.
2. Those listening should take notes on a separate piece of paper using a chart like the one on page 141.
3. At the end of the person's presentation, those listening should review their notes and each person should ask the presenter one question.
4. Repeat steps 1–3 until everyone has presented.

You mentioned that good debaters need practice learning to speak persuasively. What kind of practice do they do exactly?

Expanding Your Fluency

A Read the sayings below and then discuss the questions with a partner.

No pain, no gain.
You've got what it takes.
It's not whether you win or lose; it's how you play the game.
Practice makes perfect.
There's no *I* in *team*.
If at first you don't succeed, try, try again.
Run your own race.

1. What do you think each saying means?
2. Do you have a similar saying in your language? If so, what is it?
3. Do you agree with each saying? Why or why not?
4. Which of the sayings do you like the most and why?

B Choose one of the situations below. With a partner, create a two-minute role-play in which you use at least one of the expressions from Exercise **A**. Then do your role-play for another pair.

- You and a friend decided to take a yoga class together to get in shape. You thought the exercises would be easy, but after two weeks, you're still having a hard time getting used to them. You're feeling discouraged and are thinking about dropping the class.
- You applied for an internship with a video game company. You went on several interviews and everything went well, but the company chose someone else. You recently learned that a new position is available, but you're not sure whether to apply.
- You're working on a group project with two other people in your class. One of the people on the team is obsessed with perfection and insists on everything being done his/her way. It's driving you crazy and is making it hard for you to get motivated to do any work.

C Switch roles and repeat Exercise **B**, this time using a new scenario.

Check What You Know

Rate how well you can do the following tasks on a scale of 1–5 (5 being the best).

_________ use reported speech to explain what someone else said
_________ evaluate the relationship between activities and personal qualities
_________ pace yourself as you write a timed essay
_________ use an outline to support a presentation or essay

Pronunciation

Rising and Falling Intonation

Intonation describes the changes in pitch in spoken language. Generally, the pitch of a sentence or group of words rises or falls. The intonation tells you what kind of sentence you are hearing.

Below are the most common uses of **rising intonation**. Listen carefully to the pitch in each example. Note that it *rises* at the end of the sentence because the emphasis is on the information in the question.

- Yes–no questions with question word order:
  - May I have a glass of milk?
  - Will you help me with my chores?
- Yes–no questions with statement word order:
  - The movie starts at noon?
  - The bus station is on the corner?

Below are the most common uses of **falling intonation**. Listen carefully to the pitch in each example. Note that it *falls* at the end of the sentence. In a statement, this indicates that the sentence has ended. In *wh-* questions, the pitch is high at the beginning to emphasize the *wh-* word and falls at the end.

- Declarative statements:
  - The snow is gone.
  - The bowl is full.
- *Wh-* questions:
  - What was that noise?
  - When is the movie?

Practice

A Read and listen to each sentence. Decide if the intonation is rising or falling. Then write *rising* or *falling* on the line.

1. You are still hungry after all that pizza? ____________
2. Where are the car keys? ____________
3. Do we have homework for English class tonight? ____________
4. Everyone was late for dinner. ____________
5. Do you think that painting is beautiful? ____________
6. Are there any rooms left at the hotel? ____________
7. The ball went over the fence. ____________
8. Who was at the door? ____________

B Write three sentences of your own with rising or falling intonation. Indicate which intonation your sentence has.

1. ____
____
2. ____
____
3. ____
____

Stress Changes with Prefixes and Suffixes

In English, adding prefixes and suffixes to words does not usually cause a change in stress. Here are some examples.

different	indifferent	differently
important	unimportant	importantly
arm	disarm	disarming

However, in some cases, adding a particular suffix will cause a shift in the syllable that is stressed.

picture	picturesque

Practice

A Listen to each word pair below. Mark the stressed syllable in each word to compare stress. The first one is done for you.

1.	photograph	photographic
2.	public	publicity
3.	anticipate	anticipation
4.	care	caring
5.	correlate	correlation
6.	rhetoric	rhetorical
7.	cheer	cheerful
8.	stable	stability
9.	energy	energetic
10.	play	playing
11.	library	librarian
12.	philosophy	philosophical
13.	immediate	immediately
14.	electric	electrician
15.	hero	heroic
16.	eager	eagerly

B Now, review the stressed syllables in each word pair. Which ones changed? Which ones did not? Write a rule about which suffixes cause a stress shift.

____

____

____

Heteronyms and Stress Shift

Words with the same spelling are called **homographs**. A subset of homographs are **heteronyms**: words that are spelled the same, but are a different part of speech and are often pronounced differently.

Word	Definition	Part of speech	Stress
project	A task or work that one plans to do	noun	PROject
project	To predict	verb	proJECT

You can often differentiate between heteronyms by identifying their part of speech. For most two-syllable heteronyms, the noun has the stress on the first syllable, while the verb has the stress on the second.

Word	Definition	Part of speech	Stress
digest	A collection of readings	noun	DIgest
digest	To take in or make use of, as in a meal	verb	diGEST
entrance	An opening through which to enter	noun	ENtrance
entrance	To fill with wonder	verb	enTRANCE

Note that you cannot apply this rule to all heteronyms. For example, the verb and noun *respect / respect* are pronounced the same. Also, some heteronyms have only one syllable, such as the noun and verb *row* (ROW) / *row* (ROH). Lastly, a few heteronyms, such as *invalid / invalid*, have more than two syllables.

Practice

A **For each form of the heteronym, write the part of speech and show which syllable is stressed. The first one is done for you. Then listen to confirm your answers.**

Heteronym pair	Part of speech	Stress
1. The police arrested the **suspect** late last night.	noun	SUSpect
2. I **suspect** that dinner is going to be late tonight.		
3. You will only **compound** the problem if you try to fix the sink yourself.		
4. The scientist invented a new **compound** that might help prevent allergies.		
5. We analyzed all the data from the latest **survey**.		
6. From the top of the mountain, I was able to **survey** the land for miles around.		
7. The lawyer did not **object** to the final ruling.		
8. The **object** in the sky last night was an airplane.		
9. My roommate will not **permit** me to use her computer.		
10. If we want to go fishing, we will need a **permit**.		
11. His **conduct** during the meeting was upsetting to everyone.		
12. Our director will **conduct** the orchestra during the festival.		

Linking Sounds

In spoken English, sounds in consecutive words are linked when the final consonant in one word is followed by an initial vowel in the next word.

- I've already made my bed.
- The dog tracked mud all over the kitchen.

They are also linked when the final consonant in one word is followed by the same initial consonant in the next word.

- His shirt tore when he did a flip.
- I made dinner last night.

Practice

A **Predict where sounds are linked in each of the following sentences. Underline your predicted linking sounds. Then listen to check your predictions. Circle the linking sounds to confirm or correct your work.**

1. There was music everywhere at the fair.
2. The bell rings at the end of each class.
3. Jamie said he was sorry for calling so late.
4. The sun rises each morning at 5:00 a.m.
5. Mary didn't have enough energy to finish raking the leaves.
6. Tina left the shower running this morning.
7. She thought the painting was outstanding.
8. When we got to the zoo, the lions were being fed.
9. My sister invited me to come, too.
10. Everyone thought the play was sort of funny.

Typical Stress Patterns in Three-Syllable Words

In English, many three-syllable words follow regular stress patterns. Listen to the pronunciation of these words, noting the rhythm of each pattern. (3 = the strongest stress; 1 = the weakest stress)

3-1-1 (stress on first syllable)	1-3-1 (stress on second syllable)	3-1-2 (stress on first syllable with minor stress on third syllable)
benefit	congested	simplify
terrible	inspection	manifest

Practice

A Listen to and then repeat aloud each three-syllable word. Then write the stress pattern you hear. You may want to mark the words as you listen and speak. The first one is done for you.

1.	magnify	3-1-2
2.	beloved	
3.	genuine	
4.	telephone	
5.	audience	
6.	penetrate	
7.	specify	
8.	bicycle	
9.	operate	
10.	manager	
11.	direction	
12.	excellent	
13.	triangle	
14.	fortunate	
15.	another	

Intonation Patterns and Relative Clauses

Many English sentences can be divided into chunks with internal intonation patterns. Some relative clauses provide additional, but not crucial, information about a noun or noun phrase. This type of clause is often signaled by the words *who*, *whom*, *whose*, or *which*. It is also separated from the main part of the sentence by commas to indicate a slight pause and has its own rising and falling intonation curve. In this case, the speaker mentions that the visiting sister is from Rio, but that detail is merely informative, not critical.

My sister,/ who lives in Rio,/ is coming to visit.

Other relative clauses provide important information about the noun or noun phrase. Without this information, the meaning of the sentence might be unclear. The intonation in this case does *not* fall after "My sister," but stays the same for the whole chunk, including the defining relative clause. In this case, the speaker must have more than one sister; the intonation and punctuation clarify which sister is visiting.

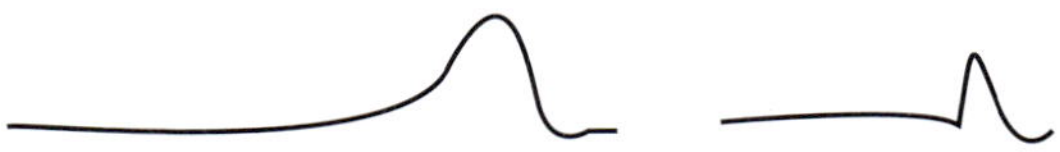

My sister who lives in Rio/ is coming to visit.

Listen to the difference between these two sentences.

- The shoes,/ which I bought yesterday,/ are the wrong color.
- The shoes that I bought yesterday/ are the wrong color.

Practice

A **Read each sentence aloud. Which segments have their own intonation curves? Separate each sentence into segments with a slash (/). Then listen to check your work. Revise your answers as necessary.**

1. Barry taught the puppy that he adopted to sit.
   Carol taught the toddler, whom she babysits, several new words.
2. The rake, which I loaned to my neighbor, broke.
   The tool that I borrowed from my father is missing.
3. Susan's new dress, which is red, is very pretty.
   The new coat that Hannah bought is beautiful.
4. Marco, who doesn't care about clothes, wears whatever fits.
   The woman who just walked by wears the coolest styles.
5. That boutique, which just opened last month, has high prices.
   The mall that opened recently is close to my house.
6. Cats that love water are very rare.
   Cats, who don't like water, are no fun to bathe.

Pronunciation

Reduction in Perfect Modals

Reduction describes the process in spoken language when sounds are shortened and, often, changed slightly. Reduction occurs only in spoken language, not in formal writing (though you may sometimes see it written, for example, in dialogues).

Perfect modals in English include *must / should / would / could* + *have* + the past participle of a verb. When spoken, the *h* in *have* is usually dropped and the vowel sound is reduced to the schwa sound or *eh*.

- You must have left the gate unlocked; that is how the dog got out. ("mustehv," not "must have")
- We should have arrived earlier. ("shouldehv," not "should have")
- She could have gotten an A on the test if she had studied harder. ("couldehv," not "could have")
- If I had known you were going, I would have attended the party, too. ("wouldehv," not "would have")

> **TIP** In very informal spoken English, perfect modals are often reduced even further to: *musteh*, *woulddeh*, *coulddeh*, and *shoulddeh*.
>
> Note that when *must have* is not followed by a past participle, it does not get reduced. For example: Bella said that she must have a new dress for the dance.

Practice

A Say each sentence aloud, and then listen to the audio recording to check your pronunciation. Then say each sentence aloud again.

1. Jane would have gone to the movies with us, but she had to work.
2. I could have ordered pizza for lunch, but had a salad instead.
3. It must have snowed two feet last night!
4. I could have done my report on climate change, but someone else chose it first.
5. Juan thought he had his wallet with him, but he must have left it at home.
6. I'm so sorry; I should have remembered your birthday!
7. Pamela would have had ice cream, but there wasn't any.
8. I sent the package, but it must have been lost in the mail.
9. Danny did everything he could have done to win the contest.
10. Callie should have called Petra last night, but she came home too late.

Thought Groups

In spoken English, longer sentences can be divided into chunks, called **thought groups**. A thought group usually contains a major element, such as a prepositional phrase, a noun phrase, or a subject / verb. Also, it is signaled by a slight pause before and after it. Lastly, a thought group is just what its name implies: a phrase that coherently expresses a thought. Fluent speakers of English pace their speech to mark thought groups, which can in turn aid comprehension, add nuance, or emphasize or deemphasize certain details. Note: there is often more than one way to divide a sentence into thought groups.

Here are some examples of thought groups within longer sentences. The groups are separated by a slash (/).

- Scientists / are doing tests / to determine how humans decide / right from wrong.
- There are special areas / of the brain / that might control moral behavior.
- These areas / are associated with emotion / and what we call *social cognition.*

Practice

A **Read each sentence aloud and separate the thought groups with a slash (/). Then listen to check your work. Revise your answers as necessary.**

1. The sun was shining this morning, but then it started to rain.
2. Perry got up late and missed his train.
3. I hope to have my project done by the end of this week.
4. Everyone really enjoyed the movie yesterday.
5. By the end of the year, we should have finished redoing the spare bedroom.
6. The price of the washing machine was less than I remembered.
7. It was cold out, but I took the dog for a walk anyway.
8. The student won an award for her environmental work.
9. Susan sat by the phone, waiting to hear if she got the job.
10. Why didn't you come to the party last night?

Language Summary

Unit 7

availability the fact that something can be used or reached **available** (adj.) **unavailable** (adj.)

bottom line the total amount of money a company has made or lost over a time

commute the daily journey you make between your home and place of work or school **to commute** (v.) **commuter** (n.)

cramped not big enough for the number of people or things in it **to cramp** (v.)

delay when you have to wait longer than expected for something to happen **to delay** (v.)

fit in to feel that you belong to a particular group and are accepted by them **misfit** (n.)

get in arrive

keep in mind to remember something important (often given as a warning/advice)

option something you can choose from a group of alternatives **to opt** (v.) **optional** (adj.)

overwhelming difficult to fight against

perfect match two things that go successfully together

pull in/pull out arrive/depart (especially used for vehicles such as trains, trucks, and cars)

punctual on time; not late **punctuality** (n.)

reliable trusted to work or behave well **to rely on** (v.) **unreliable** (adj.)

rush hour the times of day when most people are traveling to and from work

tend likely to behave in a particular way **tendency** (n.)

transfer to go or move something from one place to another

Unit 8

anonymous made or done by a person whose name is not known **anonymously** (adv.) **anonymity** (n.)

big deal something important

consequences results or effects (of an action)

criticize to express disapproval by saying what's wrong with something **critic** (n.) **criticism** (n.)

damage to harm something

discipline self-control; an action taken to correct inappropriate behavior **to discipline** (v.)

disruptive causing trouble and stopping something from continuing as usual **to disrupt** (v.) **disruption** (n.)

get away with to do something wrong or risky and not suffer any consequences

get into trouble to be in a position where you will be punished for something

get suspended temporarily not allowed to go to school or class because you've done something wrong **suspension** (n.)

goofy silly or ridiculous

illegal not allowed by law **illegally** (adv.) **legal** (adj.)

incident an event

invasion of privacy when your private life is disturbed in an unpleasant way **to invade** (v.) **invader** (n.)

private only for one person or group; not for everyone **privately** (adv.) **privacy** (n.)

punish to take action against someone for inappropriate behavior **punishment** (n.)

regulation an official rule (e.g., made by a government or school) **to regulate** (v.)

remove (a video) to delete or eliminate; **removal** (n.)

reputation the opinion that people have about someone or something; how much they respect or admire it **reputable** (adj.)

respectful to be polite and well-behaved towards someone (in authority) **(to) respect** (v., n.) **(to) disrespect** (v., n.)

responsibility something that is your job or duty to deal with **responsibly** (adv.) **responsible** (adj.)

restriction a limit on something **to restrict** (v.)

show up to appear

surveillance the careful watching of someone, especially by the police

sympathetic showing that you understand and care about someone's suffering **sympathy** (n.)

Unit 9

alert a warning, an alarm **(to) alert** (v., adj.)

attack to try to hurt someone with physical violence **attack** (n.) **attacker** (n.)

capture to catch a person or animal and confine it **capture** (n.) **captive** (adj.)

clone a genetic copy of an animal that has been made in a lab, using the DNA of another animal **to clone** (v.)

collar an item that an animal wears around its neck **to collar** (v.)

cruel very mean or unkind **cruelly** (adv.) **cruelty** (n.)

domesticated raised by people for agricultural purposes or living with people as household pets **domestication** (n.) **domestic** (adj.)

endangered in danger of dying out completely **to endanger** (v.)

evolve to slowly change and develop over time into a different form **evolution** (n.) **evolutionary** (adj.)

hunt to chase and kill an animal, usually for food **hunt** (n.) **hunter** (n.)

intercept to interrupt and stop something from happening **interception** (n.)

pesticide chemicals put on plants to kill insects

species a class of plants or animals that have the same characteristics

tag a device attached to someone or something that sounds an alarm **to tag** (v.)

train to teach a person or animal how to do something **trainee** (n.) **trainer** (n.)

treat to behave in a certain way toward someone **to mistreat** (v.) **treatment** (n.)

wild free, untamed, not taken care of by people **wildly** (adv.) **wilderness** (n.)

Unit 10

affect to influence or cause something to happen

appropriate the right or correct thing to do **appropriately** (adv.) **inappropriate** (adj.)

change (your) mind to change your decision or opinion about something

concentrate to pay close attention to something **concentration** (n.)

eager to really want to do something **eagerness** (n.)

effect the result or change that one thing causes in a second thing **side effect** (n.)

figure out to discover a solution to a problem

hesitate to not speak or act for a short time, usually because you are uncertain about something **hesitation** (n.)

impress to make someone admire you **impression** (n.) **impressive** (adj.)

intuition a feeling that something is true even when you have no proof of it **intuitively** (adv.) **intuitive** (adj.)

keep (something) in mind to remember

make up your mind to decide to do something

mature to develop **to mature** (v.)

peer someone who is your own age

process to review and consider information in order to understand it

rational logical, reasonable **rationalize** (v.) **rationally** (adv.) **irrational** (adj.)

react to respond or act in a certain way because of something that has happened **reaction** (n.)

regret to feel very sorry about the outcome of something **regret** (n.) **regretful** (adj.) **regrettable** (adj.)

speak your mind tell others honestly how you feel

Unit 11

assess to judge or decide the quality or amount of something **assessment** (n.)

batter to hit something with strong force

below freezing below the temperature at which a liquid becomes solid **to freeze** (v.) **freezing point** (n.)

boiling hot very hot **(to) boil** (v., n.)

bounce back to recover

break down to stop working properly **breakdown** (n.)

break through to emerge **breakthrough** (n.)

call off to cancel

chill out to relax

coastline the boundary between land and sea **coast** (n.) **coastal** (adj.)

cold spell when the weather suddenly gets cold and stays cold for a while **cold** (adj.)

come down to fall to the ground

come down with to get sick with a particular illness

consider to think about something carefully **consideration** (n.)

cut off to disconnect **cutoff** (n., adj.)

defend to protect someone or something against attack **defense** (n.) **defenseless** (adj.)

die down to become less

erosion the gradual removal of rock and dirt by the weather (wind, the sea, etc.) **to erode** (v.)

find out to discover

freeze up to become stuck; unable to move

frigid extremely cold

frostbite a medical condition resulting from overexposure to freezing temperatures

give up to part with; to let go of

heat stroke a medical condition resulting from overexposure to high temperatures

heatwave a period of unusually hot weather

hold off to delay, not happen immediately

ice cap a permanent covering of ice

intervene to become involved in a situation and try to change it **intervention** (n.)

look after to keep someone healthy or safe

mild moderately warm

pick up to increase

postpone to delay (an event)

put off to postpone

put up with to tolerate

recover to become well again **recovery** (n.)

refuse to decline something **refusal** (n.)

scattered showers irregular rain over an area

shrink to become smaller **shrinkage** (n.)

size up to assess

snow flurries brief, light snowfalls

step in to intervene

storm out to leave a place noisily because you're angry

take off to depart **takeoff** (n.)

think over to consider

tolerate to accept something that you may not like **tolerance** (n.) **tolerable** (adj.)

turn down to refuse

Unit 12

achieve to succeed in doing something after a lot of effort **achievement** (n.)

adjustment a change **to adjust** (v.)

beat to defeat someone in a competition **unbeatable** (adj.)

championship a competition to find the best player or team in a particular sport **champion** (n.)

coach a person who trains others to play a sport **to coach** (v.)

commitment dedication to doing something **to commit** (v.)

defend to protect from harm or injury **defense** (n.)

get used to to become accustomed to something

handful a small amount of something

in shape fit, healthy **out of shape** (adj.)

interpreter a person who translates what someone is saying into another language **to interpret** (v.) **to misinterpret** (v.)

motivation a strong desire or willingness to do something **to motivate** (v.) **motivational** (adj.)

NBA (National Basketball Association) the professional basketball organization in North America

obsessed constantly thinking about something **obsession** (n.)

opponent your rival, especially in a game **to oppose** (v.) **opposition** (n.)

physical education (PE) a school subject in which students exercise and play sports

recruit to choose and try to persuade someone to work for your organization **recruiter** (n.) **recruitment** (n.)

role model someone you admire and try to imitate

violence behavior that hurts, injures, or kills people **violently** (adv.) **violent** (adj.)

Grammar Summary

Unit 7

Comparative Forms			
	more than . . .	**less than . . .**	**equal to . . .**
Adjectives	Taking a taxi is **faster** and **more reliable than** taking the subway.	The subways are **less reliable than** they used to be. They are **not as nice as** they once were.	During rush hour, walking is **as fast as** taking the bus.
Adverbs	The trains run **faster** and **more frequently** than the bus.	The trains run **less frequently** on weekends than they do on weekdays.	The old trains run **as smoothly as** the new ones.
Noncount nouns	After I quit, I had **more time than** I used to.	As a new parent, I have **less time than** I used to.	I spend **as much** time working **as** (I did) before.
Count nouns	The local train makes **more stops than** the express (does).	The express train makes **fewer stops than** the local (does).	The Blue Line has **as many riders** as it did last year.
Irregular forms: good → better, bad → worse, far → further			

- We don't usually use *less* with one-syllable adjectives. We use *not as . . . as* instead.

  ~~*The bus is less fast than the train*~~.

  The bus is not as fast as the train.

- Here is an additional summary of comparative forms for review.

Single-syllable adjectives add *–er* (or just). If the adjective ends in a single vowel and a consonant, double the final consonant.	*clean* → *cleaner* *cute* → *cuter* *big* → *bigger*
Two-syllable adjectives ending in *–y, -le, and –ly* usually take *–er.*	*funny* → *funnier* *simple* → *simpler* *careful* → *careful*
Some adjectives can have two comparative forms.	*friendly* → *friendlier / more friendly* *happy* → *happier / more happy* *handsome* → *handsomer / more handsome*
Other adjectives with two syllables and adjectives with more than two syllables usually take *more.*	*complex* → *more complex* *intelligent* → *more intelligent* *beautiful* → *more beautiful*
Adverbs ending in *–ly* usually take *more.*	*softly* → *more softly* *quickly* → *more quickly* *regularly* → *more regularly*

Unit 8

Past Modals	
Use past modals with past participles to assess real or imaginary past actions.	
Disbelief / impossibility	Jen: Stella **couldn't have**[1] **been** texting. She lost her cell phone recently.
Possibility	Tom: She **might have**[2] **borrowed** a friend's phone to do it.
Logical conclusion	Amy: I heard she was texting her mother. It **must have been** something important.
Regret over an action that wasn't taken	Ed: Even so, she **should have waited** until after class to send a text.
Regret over an action that was taken	Mina: I agree. She **shouldn't have disrupted** the class.
[1]or *can't have*	[2]or *could have* or *may have*

- Note that while *mustn't have* is used in the context of a logical conclusion, the present/future *mustn't* is used to prohibit someone from doing something.

  You mustn't have parked on this street—I don't see you car anywhere. (logical conclusion)

  You mustn't park here because of street cleaning. (prohibition)

- As you see in the chart, *could have* is used with possibility. It can also be used in another, more subtle context: *a possibility that was not acted on* (a missed opportunity).

  Mina was late for class. She could have overslept. (It's possible the reason she was late is that she overslept; we don't know for sure).

  Mina was late for class. She could have asked me for a ride. (Mina had the option to ask for a ride, but she didn't, so she was late.)

Unit 9

Review of Passive Voice	
simple present	The animals **are** *kept* in tiny cages. It's cruel.
simple past	Dogs _______ ___________ 15,000 years ago.
present perfect	They _______ ___________ **trained** to do police and rescue work.
present continuous past continuous	The lost cat **is / was** ___________ **cared for** by a volunteer at the animal shelter.
simple future	The cat _______ **be** ___________ to its owner tomorrow.
with modals	Parrots **can** *be taught* to communicate with humans. Dogs **should** _______ ___________ on a leash.

❶ Forming the passive: Use a form of *be* + the past participle. With modals: modal + *be* + past participle

❷ To show who does the action, use *by* + noun: *The lost cat* **was found** *by a neighbor*.
If it's clear who does the action, or if it's not important, don't use *by* + noun: *Parrots* **can be taught** *to speak*.

❸ You might use the passive if:
- It's obvious who did something or the doer of the action is a general group of people: *Parrots can be taught to speak*. (We know humans are the ones teaching.)
- The action is more important than who does it: *The boy was bitten by a spider*.

- Remember, when you change a sentence from active voice to passive voice, the pronoun changes from an object pronoun to a subject pronoun.

  My friends gave ***me*** *a puppy for my birthday.*

  I *was given a puppy for my birthday.*

Grammar Summary

Unit 10

The Conditional

1. With possible (real) future events		2. With imaginary (unreal) present situations	
if *clause*	*result clause*	if *clause*	*result clause*
If I **do** that,	I'll **have** enough money	If you **had** a scholarship,	you **would have** enough money,

❶ This form of the conditional is used to make predictions and talk about possible future events. The verb in the *if* clause is in the simple present. In the result clause, the verb is in the simple future.

❷ This form of the conditional is used to talk about imaginary present events. The information in the *if* clause is not true right now. The result clause describes an imagined result. The verb in the *if* clause is in the simple past. In the result clause, *would(n't) + verb* is used. Note: *be* ➞ *were* for all subjects in the *if* clause: If I / you / he were the teacher . . .

Unit 11

Phrasal Verbs

A phrasal verb is a verb + preposition/particle. Some phrasal verbs are "separable;" the verb can be "separated" from the preposition/particle by an object (noun or a pronoun). Notice the placement of the pronoun in the separable verbs. Phrasal verbs have different meanings than the base verb on its own, as you will see in Activity **A**.

	With an object	Without an object
separable	She **gave up** her job. / She **gave** her job **up**. ~~She gave up it~~. / She **gave** it **up**. Other examples: *put off, size up, think over*	She **bounced back** (recovered) from her illness. The plane **took off** on a dangerous mission. Other examples: *die down, pick up, step in*
inseparable	She **looked after** her colleagues. The doctor **looked after** them. Other examples: *find out, put up with*	

Some phrasal verbs have three words. They are always inseparable: *How much longer do we have to* ***put up with*** *this rain? / Every winter I* ***come down with*** *a cold.*

- Phrasal verbs, like regular verbs can have more than one meaning. Some phrasal verbs can be used both transitively and intransitively.

take off

The plane eventually took off. (It left the ground.)
Her career is really taking off. (It's going well.)
He won't take his hat off. (He won't remove it.)
I took three weeks off last summer. (I had a vacation.)

Unit 12

Reported Speech

Notice! Some verbs (*convince, remind, tell*) can follow more than one pattern.

Use reported speech to explain what someone else has said. The verb tense, certain time words (such as *now, last week*), and pronouns can shift in reported speech.

Patterns in reported speech:

❶ verb + (*that*) clause: Ana **said (that) she was taking a kickboxing class.**
use with verbs: *explain, insist, mention, say*

❷ verb + pronoun/noun + (*that*) clause: Derek **told me (that) he played rugby.**
use with verbs: *convince, promise, remind, tell*

❸ verb + pronoun/noun + infinitive: Derek **encouraged his team to practice** more.
use with verbs: *beg, convince, encourage, invite, remind, tell*

Notice! Pattern 3 verbs are often used to ask for something or to give advice or instructions.

Skills Index

1B

World Class

WORKBOOK

NANCY DOUGLAS | JAMES R. MORGAN

NATIONAL GEOGRAPHIC LEARNING | CENGAGE Learning®

Australia • Brazil • Japan • Korea • Mexico • Singapore • Spain • United Kingdom • United States

CONTENTS

Credits

Photo Credits

p. 42: ©iStockphoto.com/Suprijono Suharjoto; **p. 41,** left: wavebreakmedia ltd/Shutterstock.com; **p. 41,** right: wavebreakmedia ltd/Shutterstock.com; **p. 44,** top: Graphictools/Dreamstime.com; **p. 44,** bottom: ©iStockphoto.com/Nikolajs Strigins; **p. 47:** ©iStockphoto.com/Rich Legg; **p. 50,** left (upper): Everett Collection Inc/Alamy; **p. 50,** left (lower): Gamma-Rapho via Getty Images; **p. 50,** right: Philcold/Dreamstime.com; **p. 53,** left (top): Matt Gibson/Shutterstock.com; **p. 53,** left (middle): Abramova Kseniya/Shutterstock.com; **p. 53,** left (bottom): Alekuwka/Shutterstock.com; **p. 53,** right (top): KellyNelson/Shutterstock.com; **p. 53,** right (bottom): Piyaphon/Shutterstock.com; **p. 55:** ©iStockphoto.com/Amy Smith; **p. 56:** Paul Nicklen/National Geographic Stock; **p. 60,** left: Vera Kailova/Shutterstock.com; **p. 60,** right: Anan Kaewkhammul/Shutterstock.com **p. 63:** michaeljung/Shutterstock.com; **p. 64:** ©iStockphoto.com/5D2; **p. 68,** top: oliveromg/Shutterstock.com; **p. 68,** National Geographic; **p. 69,** left to right: ©iStockphoto.com/S. Greg Panosian; ©iStockphoto.com/tirc83; ©iStockphoto.com/CountryStyle Photography; ©iStockphoto.com/mikeuk; **p. 70,** top: ©iStockphoto.com/Mac99; **p. 70,** bottom: ©iStockphoto.com/traveler1116; **p. 74,** top left: ©iStockphoto.com/Darren Mower; **p. 74,** top right: ©iStockphoto.com/Juanmonino; **p. 74,** bottom left: Feverpitched/Dreamstime.com; **p. 74,** bottom right: ©iStockphoto.com/Geir-Olav Lyngfjell; **p. 75,** left to right: ©iStockphoto.com/Christopher Futcher, Vitalii Nesterchuk/Shutterstock.com, artemisphoto/Shutterstock.com, Lucian Coman/Shutterstock.com; **p. 76:** Bernie Baker

Text Credits

Unit 7 Adapted from *Bus2Antarctica Video: Tastes Like Chicken Bus* by Andrew Evans, *Intelligent Travel*, January 10, 2010. **Unit 8** Adapted from *Pictures: 5 Cruise Ship Disasters that Changed Travel*, by Ker Than, National Geographic Daily News, January 18, 2012. **Unit 9** Adapted from *Kermode Bear* by Bruce Barcott, National Geographic Magazine, August 2011. **Unit 10** Adapted from *Swarm Theory* by Peter Miller, National Geographic Magazine, July 2007. **Unit 11** Adapted from *Changing Rains*, by Elizabeth Kolbert, National Geographic Magazine, April 2009.

7 On the Move

Unit 7 Outcomes

- make comparisons
- recognize cause-and-effect relationships
- make a complaint and propose a solution
- use facts and evidence to defend a position

Vocabulary and Grammar

A Match the words with their meanings.

1. delay ______
2. fit in ______
3. reliable ______
4. punctual ______
5. rush hour ______
6. cramped ______

a. not enough space
b. when something happens later than it should
c. when something happens on time
d. a period of heavy traffic when people go to and from work
e. to get along well with a group of people
f. dependable

B Write sentences that compare the two items mentioned based on the symbol between them and a word from the box.

comfortable	**reliable**
cramped	**slow**
fast	**stops**
punctual	**time**

Example: car > bicycle *Driving a car is faster than riding a bicycle.*

1. buses now < buses in the past ______
2. cars in rush hour = taxis in rush hour ______
3. commuter train < subway ______
4. walking > riding a bicycle ______
5. buses during rush hour = subways during rush hour ______
6. on a train > in a car ______

C Lisa and Katya are roommates. Read about their commutes. Then write three sentences that compare their commutes, using words like *more than, less than, better, worse*, etc. Be creative.

Lisa drives forty minutes to her job every day. However, it can be a bit longer sometimes because there is always traffic during rush hour. She doesn't take the bus because it is slower than driving. Plus, Lisa doesn't like to rely on a bus schedule. Parking is more expensive than a bus pass, but she doesn't mind because she can come and go as she pleases. She thinks her commute is better than Katya's.	Katya usually takes the bus to work and then transfers to the subway. It takes her forty minutes from her home to the office. She can read on the way and thinks that it is more relaxing than driving. On nice days, she often rides her bike to work. Katya checks the bus and train times on her phone and usually knows if there's a delay so she can plan accordingly. She thinks Lisa's commute is worse than hers.

1. ______
2. ______
3. ______

OUTCOME MET: make comparisons

D There are always problems with your commute to work. Write an e-mail complaining to the city's department of transportation. Mention the causes of the problem and the effects they have on your commute. Then present a solution. Use words from the box for ideas.

bad commute	**faster trains**	**reliable subway**
bike paths	**more options**	**rush hour traffic**
cramped buses	**punctual system**	**train delays**

OUTCOMES MET: recognize cause-and-effect relationships; make a complaint and propose a solution

Video

A Read the list of advantages to bike sharing. Check (✓) if it is mentioned in the video.

1. It makes commuting easier because you can eliminate transferring metro lines. ☐
2. It's perfect for taking long-distance bike trips. ☐
3. It's great for businesses to have people riding bikes down the street. ☐
4. The bikes come with a helmet for safety. ☐
5. Since everything is close by, it only takes about fifteen minutes to get somewhere by bike. ☐
6. You can bike at night because the bikes come with a built-in light. ☐
7. It is safer than taking the subway. ☐
8. What are some disadvantages to bike sharing? ____________________

____

B Think about what you know about other ways to commute. Write two sentences for each item.

1. Compare Capital Bikeshare to driving to work. ____________________

____

2. Compare Capital Bikeshare to taking the subway to work. ____________________

____

OUTCOME MET: make comparisons

Writing

City University built a new campus forty kilometers outside of the city. Almost all of its students live in the city. Only one road runs between the city and the new campus. Read the students' letters to the editor to learn of their complaints and proposed solutions for the transportation problem.

Because I don't have a car, I have been getting rides to the new campus from friends. But I have the perfect solution for you: build a subway line to the campus. The fact is that it will take five years and cost millions, but subways are faster and more reliable than buses.

The best plan is to start a bus system from the old campus to the new campus. Buses are not as fast as cars, but they save gas. This system is less expensive than the other ideas and could start immediately. Plus, students would be able to do their homework on the bus.

I can't stand traffic! Since thousands of students are driving on the small road, there are daily traffic jams. Here's my solution: build a big expressway to the new campus. It would cost millions, but other people would use it, too. It would make driving to and from the city easier.

A Write three sentences comparing the proposed solutions from the students. Use words like *more __ than, less __ than, as __ as, fewer __ than, faster, slower, better, worse, cheaper, further*, etc.

1. (bus / subway) ______________________________
2. (subway / expressway) ______________________________
3. (expressway / bus) ______________________________

OUTCOME MET: make comparisons

B What do you think would be the result of each proposed solution? Complete the chart.

Solution	Result
Build a new subway system	
Start a new bus system	
Create a new expressway	

OUTCOME MET: recognize cause-and-effect relationships

C Which solution do you think is the best (subway, bus, or expressway)? Do you have another idea? Write a letter to the Department of Transportation to propose a solution to the transportation problem. Remember to identify the problem first and present the facts. Then propose your solution.

____

____

____

____

____

____

OUTCOMES MET: make a complaint and propose a solution; use facts and evidence to defend a position

Reading

Riding Guatemala's Colorful Buses

Riding a chicken bus in Guatemala is a kind of traveler's rite of passage.[1] That people are carrying live chickens defines the bus as local and authentic.

The first bus I saw in Guatemala was in the village of La Mesilla. It was so orange and so shiny; I immediately got on it. The ticket cost me fifty quetzales (about four dollars) to ride about 200 miles into Guatemala. Upon sitting, I immediately heard the squawk[2] of a chicken. I was excited to find a real live chicken inside a bag beneath the seat in front of me.

So why do people carry chickens on buses? How many times do you carry dinner home with you? Whether in a shopping bag, in a pizza box, or in little cardboard boxes, people carry the food they eat. That's why we have chicken buses.

So many Central American buses are in fact American school buses that have undergone an extreme makeover.[3] They are covered with bright paint, wild designs, and written messages.

Driving along the steep mountain roads of Guatemala is extremely dangerous. And yet I also found comfort in knowing that these gaudy[4] buses had made the same long journey from the United States that I just did. Plus, these were the same buses that I used to ride on when I was a kid.

As the main link between remote mountain towns, Guatemala's buses are like little moving towns. They're filled with people and their things. Everyone is involved in a constant exchange of money, goods, and life.

A Guatemalan bus makes a stop at the Chichicastenango market.

Passengers themselves are in high demand. Every bus has someone that collects money, handles the luggage tied to the top of the bus, and is responsible for finding new passengers. The bus driver will wait until nearly every seat is full before departing. If you're not going to the same place, he'll still take you and your money until he meets up with another bus driver who is going where you want to go. On four different occasions I was taken off the bus with my bag and made to jump on another bus. Part of the money from my original ticket was paid to the next driver for his section of the trip. Yes, it's a confusing system, but it seems to work for them. It's also how I got across half of Guatemala in less than a day.

[1] **rite of passage** informal activity that marks an important stage or occasion in a person's life
[2] **squawk** a loud cry
[3] **makeover** a new or improved appearance that results from making many changes
[4] **gaudy** brightly colored or showily decorated to an unpleasant degree

A Complete the sentences with information about riding buses in Guatemala.

1. In order to ride two hundred miles into Guatemala, ______________________________.
2. The author heard a squawk because ______________________________.
3. People carry chickens on buses because ______________________________.
4. Guatemalan chicken buses are American school buses that ______________________________.
5. The author felt comfortable on the bus since ______________________________.
6. The author had to change buses four times because ______________________________.

OUTCOME MET: recognize cause-and-effect relationships

B Compare the bus from the reading to a different form of public transportation that you know. First, complete the chart.

	Guatemalan bus	
1. What does it look like?		
2. What is special about it?		
3. Is it dangerous?		
4. How is it similar?		
5. How is it different?		

Now write three sentences comparing them. Use words like *more __ than, less __ than, as __ as, fewer __ than, faster, slower, cheaper, better, worse, further*, etc.

1. ______________________________
2. ______________________________
3. ______________________________

OUTCOME MET: make comparisons

C You read about an adventure the author had getting from one place to another on a Guatemalan bus. Describe an interesting experience that you've had while traveling by one of these forms of transportation: *bike, boat, bus, car, motorcycle, plane, train*. Include at least one comparison.

Example: Last year I went to Montreal. I decided to get around the city by subway because it is faster than taking the bus. I was riding along when . . .

____

Outcomes

A Write a comparison between the two modes of transportation in parentheses.

Example: (local train / express train) *The local train makes more stops than the express train.*

1. (subway / taxi) ______
2. (bus / car) ______
3. (airplane / boat) ______

How did you do?: On a scale of 1–5 (with 5 being the best), how well did you **make comparisons?** ______

B Complete the sentences with your own ideas.

1. If I need to get somewhere and miss a bus, ______
2. Whenever I travel somewhere by car, I ______
3. If I call ahead of time for a taxi and it is punctual, ______
4. Because it is the most reliable option for commuting, I would take ______

How did you do?: On a scale of 1–5, how well did you **recognize cause-and-effect relationships?** ______

C You drive a large hauling truck every day for your job. You've noticed that there are more and more motorcycles on the roads that you use. They're very hard to see from your truck, and you're worried you might hit a motorcyclist one of these days. Write a complaint to local officials about all the motorcycles and propose a solution.

______
______
______
______
______
______

How did you do?: On a scale of 1–5, how well did you **make a complaint and propose a solution?** ______

D Your city has a lot of traffic problems and is adding a tax for car ownership. The tax will encourage more people to use public transportation, and the money will be used to improve both the roads and the subways. However, the tax is quite expensive and will be difficult for many people to pay. State a position on the issue. Then write three facts to defend it.

Your position on the new tax: ______

1. ______
2. ______
3. ______

How did you do?: On a scale of 1–5, how well did you **use facts and evidence to defend a position?** ______

8 Think Twice

Vocabulary and Grammar

Unit 8 Outcomes

- use past modals to consider possibilities,express disbelief and regret, and make logical conclusions
- compare actions to their consequences
- recognize hardship and express sympathy
- respond to a news story with your own opinion

A Complete the list of rules at a movie theater with the words from the box. Two will not be used.

consequences	**disruptive**	**get into trouble**	**respectful**
discipline	**get away with**	**regulations**	**restrictions**

1. Be polite and ______________________ of other people in the theater.
2. One good way to ______________________ is if you talk on your cell phone during a movie. Turn them off!
3. You won't be able to ______________________ smoking, so don't even think about it.
4. The ______________________ for rude behavior is that you will be asked to leave the theater and, of course, miss a really great movie!
5. Because of the age ______________________ on certain films, you may be required to show identification.
6. If you follow all of the above ______________________, we promise you'll enjoy your movie-going experience!

B A man sitting next to you at a movie theater was very disruptive. He talked loudly on the phone, sent text messages, and kept getting in and out of his seat. Complete the sentences using past modals.

Example: You wouldn't believe this guy talking on his phone during the movie. He *must have thought* he was the only person in the theater.

1. He ______________________ turned off his phone.
2. He ______________________ disrupted the movie.
3. I ______________________ asked him politely to be quiet.
4. I ______________________ yelled at him, because then I disrupted the movie!
5. I suppose I ______________________ moved to a different seat, but I was annoyed.
6. I mean, I heard him talking about a baseball game, so it ______________________ an important conversation.

OUTCOME MET: use past modals to consider possibilities

C Read the news story and complete the items on the following page.

Ryan Braun, a Major League Baseball player for the Milwaukee Brewers, is considered to be one of the best young players in the game. He won the Most Valuable Player award for his performance during the 2011 season. But late in the same year, it was reported that Braun tested positive for a performance-enhancing drug (PED). A PED is any substance that is believed to make players stronger or faster, and baseball regulations ban these substances. The consequence for testing positive for a PED is that a player cannot play for fifty games. Braun claims that he has never taken PEDs and that he is innocent. Major League Baseball reviewed the evidence and decided that Braun would not have to sit out for fifty games. But fans are left to wonder if he really is innocent or if he is getting away with breaking the rules.

React to the statements from the news story with your opinions. Use past modals when possible.

1. Ryan Braun won the Most Valuable Player award in 2011. ______________________
2. Braun tested positive for a performance-enhancing drug. ______________________
3. Baseball regulations ban the use of PEDs. ______________________
4. Braun claims that he has never taken PEDs and that he is innocent. ______________________
5. Major League Baseball decided that Braun would not have to sit out for fifty games.

____

OUTCOME MET: respond to a news story with your own opinion

Video

A Watch the video and complete the sentences with words from the box. Two words will not be used.

click	embarrassing	name	reputation	restriction
control	funny	privately	responsibility	search

1. Before the days of the Internet, ______________ moments didn't last.
2. ______________ engines scan all images, words, and videos and save them for search results.
3. If you share a video that makes someone look bad, it could damage his or her ______________.
4. Once you upload a photo and hit "click," you lose ______________ of who can see it on the Web.
5. There are ways to share information ______________ without having it scanned.
6. It's better to avoid using someone's ______________ since it's easy for the Web to scan.
7. It's important for you and your friends to take ______________ for what you post.
8. You should always think before you ______________.

B The video explains the dangers of putting information online. Now read about an online post and answer the questions with complete sentences.

Lorenzo's father owns a popular pizza place called Romano's. A new pizza restaurant, The Biggest Slice, opened nearby, and the family is worried about the competition. So, Lorenzo posted a bad review of the new restaurant on a food Web site. None of his comments were true! Now he regrets his actions.

1. What do you think about what Lorenzo did? Explain your answer.

____

2. What could he have done instead?

____

3. What might be the consequences of his actions?

____

4. What do you think he should do to fix his mistake?

____

OUTCOME MET: compare actions to their consequences

Writing

I was a crewmember on board the SS Morro Castle. It started off as a fun adventure. I had a great time with my crewmates, but we didn't follow the rules. My mates misbehaved and seemed to get away with it. I should've paid more attention to Harry. He was the only one who seemed unhappy. He never listened to the captain's orders and was the only one who got into trouble. Harry must have been mad that he had been singled out. So he went into his room, lit a match, and dropped it in a wastebasket. By the time I realized that he was missing, the fire had spread! It was a terrible fire. My biggest regret is that I could have prevented it if I had checked on Harry. I would like to tell the families of those who died how sorry I am for their loss.

A Answer the questions.

1. What past modals appear in the journal? ______
2. Who caused the fire? How? ______
3. What would the author like to tell the families of the people who died? ______

______

B The article on page 50 is about disasters on three ships. Imagine that you were the captain, a crewmember, or a passenger on one of the ships. Organize your ideas by completing the sentences.

1. I was ______ on the ship.
2. As a result of ______, we ______.
3. After the disaster, we ______.
4. I could have ______.
5. I shouldn't have ______.
6. I feel ______.
7. I'm sorry that ______.
8. I should have ______.

C Now write the story of what happened to you on the ship. Use at least four ideas from Exercise **B**. Add your own ideas and express your feelings of regret, disbelief, anger, or sympathy.

______
______
______
______
______
______
______
______
______

OUTCOMES MET: use past modals to consider possibilities, express disbelief and regret, and make logical conclusions; compare actions to their consequences; recognize hardship and express sympathy; respond to a news story with your own opinion

Reading

Cruise Ship Disasters That Changed Travel

Titanic

More than 1,500 people died when the *Titanic* sank. When the *Titanic* left Southampton, it only had enough lifeboats for about half the people on board. Also, no lifeboat drill involving passengers was performed before the *Titanic* set out. In the few lifeboats that were available, many of the oars were so new that they were still tied with string. As a result of the *Titanic* disaster, modern cruise ships now must carry enough lifeboats for all of the passengers on board.

Many observers and survivors of the *Costa Concordia* accident have compared it to the *Titanic* disaster. Some of those comparisons are correct, said Robert Ballard, who discovered the wreck of the *Titanic* in 1985. "Both of their captains showed poor judgment," Ballard said.

The RMS *Titanic* sank in the North Atlantic Ocean during the ship's first voyage from Southampton, UK, to New York City on April 15, 1912.

SS *Morro Castle*

The SS *Morro Castle* was sailing from New York City to Havana, Cuba, in 1934 when it caught fire. The ship eventually made it to Asbury Park, New Jersey, where it went onto the shore.

The cause of the fire is unclear. Most experts agree that poor crew discipline was partly to blame. "Some said she caught fire because of unhappy or vengeful[1] crewmen," historian John Maxtone-Graham said. "There was a story—and I can't say this was true—that there was a fire in a wastebasket and a crewman put it in a closet, shut the door, and went about his business."

As a result of the *Morro Castle* disaster, cruise companies began to pay more attention to training the crew to ensure proper behavior, he added. In addition, regulations were made requiring ships to be built using materials that don't burn as easily.

The SS *Morro Castle* cruise ship caught fire on September 8, 1934.

Costa Concordia

The *Costa Concordia* cruise ship was badly damaged after it hit some rocks close to shore in January 2012. The ship's captain had steered the 126,000-ton ship very close to the island of Giglio. Sources say that he was trying to greet people on the island.

Rescuers confirmed that twenty-five people died in the accident and seven people were missing. The captain of the ship was accused of manslaughter,[2] causing a shipwreck, and abandoning[3] ship.

Maxtone-Graham said the decision by the captain to leave the sinking ship early was shameful. The captain is always supposed to be the last one off a sinking ship after all the passengers get off safely.

Unlike the disasters of the *Titanic* and the SS *Morro Castle*, the *Costa Concordia* incident happened during the information age. The Internet and twenty-four-hour news cycles kept the world informed of the accident and the questionable actions of the ship's captain as they happened. Nowadays, it's harder than it used to be to escape the consequences of a disaster at sea.

The cruise ship *Costa Concordia* lies partially sunk near Italy on January 13, 2012.

[1] **vengeful** wanting to harm someone who wronged you
[2] **manslaughter** an action that results in the unintentional death of others
[3] **abandoning** leaving

A Write what happened as a result of each action.

1. Since there were not enough lifeboats on the *Titanic*, ____________________.
2. Possibly because of a fire in a wastebasket, the SS *Morro Castle* ____________________.
3. As a result of the SS *Morro Castle* disaster, ____________________.
4. A positive outcome of the *Titanic* disaster is that ____________________.
5. When the captain of the *Costa Concordia* steered the boat too close to shore, ____________________.
6. Because the captain of the *Costa Concordia* did not return to the ship, ____________________.

OUTCOME MET: compare actions to their consequences

B Answer the questions with complete sentences.

1. What could have been done to prevent such a terrible disaster on the *Titanic*?

   ____

2. What must have happened on the SS *Morro Castle* for a crew member to want to start a fire?

   ____

3. What should the captain of the *Costa Concordia* have done once it hit the ground?

   ____

OUTCOME MET: use past modals to consider possibilities, express disbelief and regret, and make logical conclusions

C Imagine that you are a politician who must write a letter to the family of a victim of one of the ship disasters you read about. First, express your sympathies to the family. Then, use past modals to express your feelings about what happened. Finally, tell the family what you will do as a leader to make sure something like this doesn't happen again. Use words from the box.

consequences	**get away with**	**punish**	**restriction**
discipline	**get into trouble**	**regulation**	**sorry**

____

____

____

____

____

____

____

____

____

____

____

____

OUTCOMES MET: use past modals to consider possibilities, express disbelief and regret, and make logical conclusions; recognize hardship and express sympathy; respond to a news story with your own opinion

Outcomes

A Write reactions to each situation using past modals.

1. You missed your friend's birthday party. You've called and left several messages, but she hasn't called you back.
 ______
2. You thought you saw your brother at the mall today, but you know he has class at that time.
 ______
3. You spent all your money on a new outfit, and now you have a big credit card bill.
 ______
4. You promised your friend you'd help him with a homework assignment, but he hasn't called.
 ______

How did you do?: On a scale of 1–5 (with 5 being the best), how well did you **use past modals to consider possibilities, express disbelief and regret, and make logical conclusions?** ______

B Write a possible consequence for each action.

1. You went to a party last night instead of studying for today's test. ______
 ______
2. You didn't talk to your best friend on his or her birthday. ______
 ______
3. You borrowed your father's cell phone and lost it. ______
 ______

How did you do?: On a scale of 1–5, how well did you **compare actions to their consequences?** ______

C Your friend Gio was recently in a bad car accident and is recovering in the hospital. Write a card to him that mentions what he's going through and expresses your sympathy.

______
______
______
______

How did you do?: On a scale of 1–5, how well did you **recognize hardship and express sympathy**? ______

D Reread the news story about the baseball player Ryan Braun on page 48. What do you think about his actions? Write a paragraph with your opinion.

______
______
______
______

How did you do?: On a scale of 1–5, how well did you **respond to a news story with your own opinion?** ______

9 In the Wild

Vocabulary and Grammar

Unit 9 Outcomes

- use different forms of the passive voice
- use an outline to summarize ideas
- raise people's awareness about an issue
- write strong sentences to capture your readers' attention

A Write a complete sentence about each picture using words from the box.

attack	**cruel**	**endangered**	**species**	**treat**
capture	**domesticated**	**hunt**	**train**	**wild**

Example: *The wild elephants are walking near a beautiful lake at sunset.*

1. ____________________

2. ____________________

3. ____________________

4. ____________________

B **Rewrite the underlined sentences using the passive voice.**

1. Alfredo was a stray dog living on the streets. Sometimes other dogs attacked him.
____
2. Animal Rescue captured him and brought him to a shelter. He wasn't very happy there.
____
3. A couple came into the shelter and decided to adopt Alfredo. A dog trainer will train him.
____
4. Jeff and Nancy are now taking care of him. He's quite happy.
____
5. Their two daughters are treating him very well. They enjoy playing with him in the backyard.
____

C Read the e-mail and complete the blanks with the correct form of the passive voice.

Send Chat Attach Address Font Colors Save as Draft

To: diego@email.com

Subject: Wild animals in the neighborhood!

As you know, each year, a pool party (1) ____________________ (*present:* hold) in my neighborhood. It is always so much fun! The weather was great this year, and we were all outside. The food (2) ____________________ (*past:* serve), and everyone was having a good time.

All of a sudden, a wild turkey ran by us, and it (3) ____________________ (*past continuous:* chase) by a coyote! Both animals ran through a gate (4) ____________________ (*past:* leave) open in somebody's back yard. One of the neighbors acted quickly and closed the gate. The coyote then lost interest in the turkey and realized it (5) ____________________ (*past:* trap), so it jumped over the fence and disappeared. The turkey couldn't jump that high, so it ran all around the yard flapping its wings. Several neighbors tried to corner it, but the turkey (6) ____________________ (*past modal:* capture). Luckily, my friend Vince, who was at the party, is a veterinarian, and all veterinarians (7) ____________________ (*present perfect:* trained) to rescue animals. He announced to everyone, "The turkey (8) ____________________ (*simple future:* catch) only if everyone stays calm and stops moving." So everyone did, and sure enough, Vince captured the turkey. Its wing (9) ____________________ (*past:* injure) by the coyote, so it's now (10) ____________________ (*present continuous:* take care of) by the local animal hospital.

What a party, huh?
Thea

OUTCOME MET: use different forms of the passive voice

Video

A Watch the video and number the events in order from 1 to 8 according to the video.

______ Now Daballen has only twenty minutes to attach the collar.

______ If the elephant crosses a virtual fence line, her collar will send a text message to a server.

______ They identify a female elephant that will be collared.

______ Then the server sends text alerts to a list of recipients who can stop the herd before it gets to a farm.

______ Ian Douglas Hamilton is in the air and David Daballen is on the ground searching for a herd.

______ Once the collar is on, the elephant will be able to communicate with them.

______ Ian sees two groups of elephants under the trees.

______ They shoot her with a tranquilizer gun.

B You are part of Hamilton and Daballen's team. Write four sentences to make others aware of what is happening to the elephants and to inform others about the benefits of "geo-fencing."

1. ______________________________
2. ______________________________
3. ______________________________
4. ______________________________

OUTCOME MET: raise people's awareness about an issue

Writing

In favor of zoos	Against zoos
1. Many endangered species are protected by zoos. 2. Zoos help us understand and study animals. 3. In the zoo, animals are well fed and well taken care of by zookeepers. 4. Zoos are educational places where children can learn about conservation and endangered species.	1. By nature, animals are wild. They should live in the wild. 2. Scientists can study animals in the wild. We have new technology to help. 3. Animals can hunt and defend themselves in the wild. 4. Because the zoo setting is artificial, children don't really see what the natural environment is like.

A Read the pros and cons about zoos. Then choose a column and add to the list by writing three of your own ideas.

1. ______________________________
2. ______________________________
3. ______________________________

B Your city wants to build a zoo near your neighborhood. Are you in favor of the zoo or against it? Using the list and your own thoughts from Exercise **A**, summarize your ideas in an outline.

1. (intro: main idea) ______________________________
   A. ______________________________
   B. ______________________________
2. (body: main idea) ______________________________
   A. ______________________________
   B. ______________________________
3. (conclusion: main idea) ______________________________
   A. ______________________________
   B. ______________________________

OUTCOME MET: use an outline to summarize ideas

C Write an essay about whether or not you think that they should build a zoo near you. Use your ideas from Exercises **A** and **B** in your writing. Remember that you want to capture your readers' attention.

____

____

____

____

____

____

OUTCOME MET: write strong sentences to capture your readers' attention

Reading

Spirit Bear

Neither albino[1] nor polar bear, the spirit bear (also known as the Kermode bear) is a white variation of the North American black bear. It's found in the Great Bear Rainforest. At 25,000 square miles—one and a half times as big as Switzerland—the region runs 250 miles down Canada's western coast. Black bears, wolves, wolverines, and whales live along a coast that has been home to First Nations[2] like the Gitga'at for hundreds of generations. It's a wild, mysterious place: There are wolves here that fish. Deer that swim. Western red cedar trees that have stood a thousand years or more. And a black bear that is white.

In a moss-covered rain forest in British Columbia, tall red cedars live a thousand years, and black bears are born with white fur.

"Our people never hunted the white bear," says Helen Clifton. Strong in voice and spirit, the 86-year-old Clifton is a clan matriarch[3] of the Gitga'at. The Gitga'at are one of fourteen groups that make up the Tsimshian people of British Columbia's northwest coast. Bear meat was rarely a main food, she says. But First Nations hunters went after black bear in greater numbers when European traders established the British Columbian fur trade in the late eighteenth century. Even in those days, taking a white bear was prohibited, a tradition that has continued through many generations. "We never even spoke of the spirit bear at the dinner table," Clifton says.

That tight-lipped[4] tradition might have been an early form of environmental protection. By not speaking of the bear, much less hunting it, the Gitga'at and neighboring bands never let word of the animal reach the ears of fur traders. Even today the Gitga'at and Kitasoo/Xai'xais people keep a watchful eye on their bears during hunting season.

That attitude makes a difference. For decades the presence of legal and illegal hunters—as well as processing plants and a factory—made grizzlies in the Great Bear Rainforest a rare sight. The industries are now gone, as is the grizzly hunt in parts of the rain forest. The bears are responding. "In my early years it was really something to see a grizzly bear," Doug Stewart tells me. As a fisheries patrolman, Stewart has been monitoring fish in the Great Bear for over thirty-five years. "Now you see them all the time. I may come across five grizzlies in a morning."

The islands do offer something else: the eyes of humans watching over them. "I tell the younger people," says Helen Clifton, "when you see a spirit bear, don't get on the VHF [radio] and broadcast it. If you want to tell someone, say you saw *mooksgm'ol*. They'll know what you mean. And it'll keep the bears safe."

[1] **albino** abnormally white or milky
[2] **First Nations** communities of indigenous people descended from the people who inhabited Canada before the European settlers arrived
[3] **clan matriarch** woman head of the clan (group of families related through a common ancestor or marriage)
[4] **tight-lipped** unwilling to talk

A Complete the outline with information from the reading.

Paragraph 1: The ___________ bear

A. It is a white variation of the ___________.

B. It lives in ___________.

Paragraph 2: Hunting

A. Helen Clifton, from the Gitga'at clan, said that ___________ was not a main food.

B. Hunters went after the black bear, but the ___________.

Paragraph 3: An early ___________ protection

A. Because they did not ___________, they were protecting them from hunters.

Paragraph 4: More bears in the woods

A. Many of the ___________ are now gone.

B. Now it is much easier to ___________.

Paragraph 5: How they keep the bears ___________

A. Helen Clifton tells younger people not to ___________.

B. They refer to the bears as *mooksgm'ol* instead of calling them ___________.

B Answer the questions about the reading with complete sentences.

1. What is different about the wolves and deer that live in the Great Bear Rainforest?

____

____

2. Who hunted the black bears? Why?

____

____

3. Who protects the Kermode bears? How?

____

____

C You are a part of the Gitga'at group of people. Write a short paragraph to explain why you think it is important to protect the Kermode bears.

____

____

____

____

____

____

____

____

____

____

____

____

____

Outcomes

A Write sentences with the passive voice based on the prompts.

1. (present perfect) ape / capture / scientist
____
2. (simple past) mouse / chase / cat
____
3. (present continuous) turtle / care for / students in the class
____
4. (simple future) elephant / train / zookeeper
____
5. (simple present) sheep / raise / farmer
____

How did you do?: On a scale of 1–5 (with 5 being the best), how well did you **use different forms of the passive voice?** _____

B Refer to the outline you created on page 55. Create a new outline in which you take the *opposite* point of view about having a zoo in the neighborhood.

1. (intro: main idea) _______________
   A. _______________
   B. _______________
2. (body: main idea) _______________
   A. _______________
   B. _______________
3. (conclusion: main idea) _______________
   A. _______________
   B. _______________

How did you do?: On a scale of 1–5, how well did you **use an outline to summarize ideas**? _____

C Write about an endangered animal for a brochure. Explain why it is endangered and what can be done to help protect it. The brochure should be worded to capture readers' attention. Use words in the box for ideas.

attack	**hunt**
capture	**species**
cruel	**train**
domesticated	**treat**
endangered	**wild**

____
____
____
____
____
____
____

How did you do?: On a scale of 1–5, how well did you **raise people's awareness about an issue?** _____
On a scale of 1–5, how well did you **write strong sentences to capture your readers' attention?** _____

7–9 Review

Vocabulary Review

A Match the word or phrase on the left with its opposite meaning on the right.

1. delay ______	6. cruel ______	a. spacious	f. kind
2. endangered ______	7. criticize ______	b. impolite	g. wild
3. fit in ______	8. domesticated ______	c. don't belong	h. on time
4. cramped ______	9. get away with ______	d. praise	i. get into trouble
5. capture ______	10. respectful ______	e. plentiful	j. set free

B Circle the word or phrase that does not belong in each group.

1. fit in	punish	get into trouble	consequences
2. rush hour	restriction	commute	cramped
3. attack	hunt	evolve	capture
4. animal	endangered	species	punctual
5. regulation	restriction	wild	limit
6. punctual	reliable	disruptive	on time

C Write sentences about yourself and people you know, using words from the box.

commute	**disruptive**	**overwhelming**	**respectful**	**transfer**
cruel	**get away with**	**reliable**	**tend**	**treat**

Example: *It's disruptive when my friend Karen sends texts during class.*

1. ______________________________
2. ______________________________
3. ______________________________
4. ______________________________

D Think of a time when someone you know did not follow the rules. Then answer the questions with complete sentences.

1. What rule or regulation was broken? How?
____
2. Did he or she get away with it or get into trouble?
____
3. How was he or she treated? ______________________________
4. Were there any consequences? ______________________________

Grammar Review

A Circle the correct answer.

1. Reeya got to class late today. She should have / must have slept late.
2. I'm not sure where she is now. She might have / should have gone to get a coffee.
3. It was distracting when Marta texted during class. She must have / should have waited until after class.
4. Marta is a good / better student than Brian.
5. I take the subway to campus. It is faster and more reliable / as fast and as reliable than taking the bus.
6. The bus makes as many / more stops than the subway. It's much slower.
7. I think that I should be allowed / should allow to bring my dog to class. I bring him everywhere I go.
8. Do you think it's unfair for a dog to be treated / is treated better than a person?

B Read the information. Then write four comparisons about the animals using words like *more than, less than, better, worse, faster, slower, bigger, smaller, as . . . as*, etc.

CHESTER THE CAT

- lives with his owners in a small house
- weighs 4 kilograms and is 24 centimeters long
- loves his owners and is quite social
- hates water and never swims
- mostly eats wet and dry cat food
- found a mouse once and hunted him down
- can run about 30 kilometers per hour

SAM THE TIGER

- lives in the wild; territory covers 70 kilometers
- weighs 200 kilograms and is 2.5 meters long
- leads a mostly solitary life
- swims and bathes in nearby ponds
- mostly eats medium-sized animals and prefers to hunt at night
- can run about 49 kilometers per hour

Example: *Chester is smaller than Sam.*

1. ____________________
2. ____________________
3. ____________________
4. ____________________

C Think of a time when you did not follow the rules. Write an e-mail to a friend telling the story. You can use your answers from Exercise **D** on page 59 for ideas. Be sure to:

- Write two sentences using the passive voice (use a form of *be* + the past participle).
- Write two sentences using past modals (*could / couldn't have; should / shouldn't have / must have*).

10 Decisions, Decisions

Vocabulary and Grammar

Unit 10 Outcomes

- use the conditional to make predictions and talk about hypothetical situations
- identify cause and effect relationships
- identify factors that influence decisions
- give reasons to justify a decision

A Complete the text messages with the correct vocabulary words or expressions from the box. Two will not be used.

affect	**concentrate**	**figure out**	**process**
change your mind	**effect**	**hesitate**	**regret**

Did you (1) ________________ about going to the concert tonight?

I would love to go, but I have to (2) ________________ on biology. I have a midterm next week. ☹

It's Saturday. You still have a few days to study. If you don't come, you may (3) ________________ it. Smash It Up is your favorite band! ☺

I know! But I can't decide right now. I need to (4) ________________ if I'll have enough time to finish three chapters.

Would it (5) ________________ your decision if I remind you that Monday is a holiday?

It is?! I totally forgot … So I have an extra day to study? I am there!

Yay! ☺ Don't (6) ________________! Close your book and get over here!

On my way!

B Match the cause on the left to the effect on the right.

1. Because Marta stayed up all night, ______
2. Since Susanne spent two hours doing homework, ______
3. Julie's favorite soccer team lost the big game, so ______
4. Silvia wrote a negative blog about her friend and ______
5. Because Linda needed help writing her essay, ______

a. then she regretted hurting her feelings.
b. her teacher did not hesitate to offer writing tips.
c. she reacted by yelling at the TV.
d. she had trouble concentrating the next day.
e. she was able to figure out all of the answers.

OUTCOME MET: identify cause and effect relationships

C Complete the sentences with your own ideas. Remember to use the correct verb forms.

Example: If I had a million dollars, I would travel around the world.

1. If I found a wallet full of money on the train, ____________________.
2. If we go out tonight, ____________________.
3. I would have more money if ____________________.
4. If the weather is nice tomorrow, ____________________.
5. If my friends don't have plans on Saturday, ____________________.

OUTCOME MET: use the conditional to make predictions and talk about hypothetical situations

Video

A Watch the video. Check (✓) the sentences that are true. Correct the false sentences.

1. ( ) Tyler is put into a scanner to help the scientists see how he will handle a simple dilemma.
2. ( ) Tyler must decide whether or not to help an injured woman.
3. ( ) Tyler takes a very long time to make a decision.
4. ( ) Tyler's answer is different from what most people who take the test say.
5. ( ) The majority of people say that it's okay to leave her behind.
6. ( ) The test shows more activity in parts of the brain that are associated with emotion.
7. ( ) The scientists don't feel that Tyler's intuitive emotional response is what guided him in his decision.

B Answer the questions in complete sentences based on the video and your own ideas.

1. What was Tyler's decision?
2. Why did he make that choice? Give two possible reasons.
3. Did he make the appropriate decision? Explain your answer in two or three sentences.

OUTCOMES MET: identify factors that influence decisions; give reasons to justify a decision

Writing

Imagine that you could make one wish to have any talent, skill, or ability, and it would come true. What would you wish for?

If I could have any talent, I would wish to be a master chef. As a chef, I would be able to create delicious meals. I would have a popular restaurant in New York City, and all of my friends and family would eat there. They would love it! However, I would have to work at night and on the weekends, so they would probably miss spending time with me.

The reason why I would choose to be a chef is because I am a terrible cook. Usually I end up burning dinner or making food that is too salty to eat. Several times a week, I end up ordering takeout from a restaurant instead of cooking. If I were a master chef, all of my meals would be delicious!

A Brainstorm a list of talents, skills, or abilities that you would like to master (*singing, speaking another language, mountain climbing,* etc.). Include one or two reasons why you wish you could do each one.

talent / skill / ability	Reasons
1.	
2.	
3.	
4.	

B Choose one of the talents, skills, or abilities you wrote about in Exercise **A**. Imagine if you were granted your wish. How would it affect your friends and family?

Example: If I were a master chef, my friends and family would love eating in my restaurant. However, I would have to work at night and on the weekends, so they would probably miss spending time with me.

____

____

____

OUTCOME MET: identify cause and effect relationships

C Which talent, skill, or ability would you choose if you were granted your wish? Write a paragraph describing what you would do and how it would change your life. Remember to use the conditional to talk about hypothetical situations.

____

____

____

____

____

____

____

OUTCOME MET: use the conditional to make predictions and talk about hypothetical situations

Reading

Thinking Like Bees

Scientist Thomas Seeley has been studying the ability of honeybees to make good decisions. In a hive of honeybees, there are as many as 50,000 individual worker bees.[1] These bees have developed ways to work through differences of opinion to do what's best for the colony.[2] People can learn a lot from bees. If people could be as effective in offices and town meetings, Seeley says, we could avoid problems making decisions.

Seeley and others are especially interested in how colonies of honeybees choose a new home. In late spring, when a hive gets too crowded, a colony usually divides. The queen bee (the leader of the hive), some male bees, and about half the workers fly away and meet again on a tree branch. Most of the bees wait there for a short time. A few other bees search for a new place to live. The best home will be a hole in a tree, high off the ground. The new hive will have lots of room inside for young bees and honey. Once a colony chooses a place, it usually won't move again. It has to make the right choice.

A swarm of honeybees in a hive.

The bees have rules for making decisions. Small groups look for different places where they could live. They do dances to compete for the best idea. Then they narrow choices by gathering at the site they like best. Seeley is impressed with the bees' rules for making decisions. He now uses them at his university, where he is head of his department.

"I've applied what I've learned from the bees to run faculty[3] meetings," he says. He tries not to make a decision before going to a meeting. He wants to hear what others say. And he does not want to pressure people to agree. Seeley asks his group to talk about the possible options, discuss their ideas, and then make a secret vote. "It's exactly what the swarm bees do, which gives a group time to let the best ideas emerge[4] and win."

In fact, almost any group that follows the bees' rules will make itself smarter, says James Surowiecki, author of *The Wisdom of Crowds*. "The bees are predicting which nest site will be best, and humans can do the same thing." If members of a group are diverse, think for themselves, and can reach a group decision, they can be smart groups, too.

[1] **worker bees** insects in a hive that carry out the work, like gathering food
[2] **colony** a group of bees living together
[3] **faculty** the teaching staff for a university department
[4] **emerge** appear; come out

A Match the information to make true sentences based on the reading.

1. Honeybees have found ways to work through differences of opinion in order to ______.
2. If people imitated the ways bees make decisions, they could be more ______.
3. Because Seeley was so impressed by the bees' rules for making decisions, he ______.
4. It's important for bees to make the right choice about a site for a home because ______.
5. James Surowiecki feels that almost any group that follows the bees' rules ______.
6. Groups that make smart decisions should be diverse, have members that think for themselves, and ______.

a. uses them at work
b. be able to reach a group decision
c. effective in offices or other meetings
d. will become smarter
e. do what's best for the group
f. they won't move once they choose it

B Answer the questions in complete sentences.

1. How do bees make decisions?

____

____

2. How do people make decisions?

____

____

3. Do you think that bee behavior is a good model for making decisions? Explain your answer.

____

____

OUTCOME MET: identify factors that influence decisions

C Imagine that your teacher is planning to give you a midterm exam but can't decide whether it should happen before a two-week break or after. Your teacher is leaving it up to the class to decide. Using the bees' decision-making process as a model, explain how you and your classmates would decide what to do and why.

____

____

____

____

____

____

____

____

____

____

OUTCOMES MET: use the conditional to make predictions and talk about hypothetical situations; identify factors that influence decisions; give reasons to justify a decision

Outcomes

A Complete the sentences with your own ideas.

1. If I lost my wallet, I ______________________
2. If I were a super hero, I ______________________
3. If I won the lottery, I ______________________
4. If I were stuck on an elevator, I ______________________

How did you do?: On a scale of 1–5 (with 5 being the best), how well did you **use the conditional to make predictions and talk about hypothetical situations**? ______

B Write a missing cause or effect in the chart.

Cause	Effect
1. Because I stayed up all night,	
2.	I was late to the movies.
3.	we lost the game.
4. Since I burned dinner,	

How did you do?: On a scale of 1–5, how well did you **identify cause and effect relationships**? ______

C Think about a decision you made recently. Name four factors that influenced your decision.

1. ______________________
2. ______________________
3. ______________________
4. ______________________

How did you do?: On a scale of 1–5, how well did you **identify factors that influence decisions**? ______

D Why did you decide to study English? Write a short paragraph and give at least two reasons that you're learning English.

____

____

____

____

____

How did you do?: On a scale of 1–5, how well did you **give reasons to justify a decision**? ______

11 Rain or Shine

Vocabulary and Grammar

Unit 11 Outcomes

- explain how weather affects your life
- make inferences based on information you have learned
- understand and use similes
- use phrasal verbs

A Complete the dialogue with the correct vocabulary words or expressions from the box. One will not be used.

consider	freezing	look after	postponed	take off
cut off	frigid	mild	refuse	tolerate

Peter: What are you doing on the computer?

Marcos: Checking my sister's flight status. With this snowstorm, I hope her flight hasn't been (1) ____________.

Peter: What time is her flight supposed to (2) ____________?

Marcos: At ten.

Peter: Did you (3) ____________ calling her cell phone?

Marcos: I tried. We talked for a minute, but got (4) ____________.

Peter: That's too bad. Why don't you check a weather Web site? Isn't the weather much more (5) ____________ where she lives? Maybe she won't have a problem leaving.

Marcos: That's true. It's just (6) ____________ outside. Look at all that snow and wind! Even if she makes it, I don't know how she'll (7) ____________ the weather up here.

Peter: Why didn't you go there instead?

Marcos: The airfare to fly north in the winter is much more reasonable, so I paid for her ticket. Julia couldn't (8) ____________ that offer.

Peter: That makes sense. I mean, who would want to come to this (9) ____________ area if they didn't have to?

B Jana writes a travel journal about a trip with her friend Daiva. Choose the correct verb for each sentence. One verb will be used twice.

1. I ______ up at 7:00 a.m. and look out the window. It's another rainy day!
2. I can't find my umbrella. I have to ______ for it before Daiva comes.
3. Daiva ______ me up at 7:45 a.m.
4. The bus ______ off at 8:45 a.m. It may be a slow ride because of the rain.
5. It's warm on the bus. I ______ off my raincoat.
6. I like to ______ out with Daiva. She's a lot of fun.
7. Daiva's music is so loud. I asked her to ______ it down a little.
8. It's time to ______ off the bus. Ugh! It's pouring outside.
9. We need to ______ after each other in the city so we can stay safe.

a. picks
b. hang
c. wake
d. turn
e. takes
f. get
g. look
h. take

OUTCOME MET: use phrasal verbs

C Think of a time you had to change your plans because of the weather. Write a paragraph about it. Use two words or expressions from each group.

Group A		Group B	
assess	postpone	cut off	give up
consider	refuse	fall through	pick up
intervene	tolerate	figure out	put up with

OUTCOMES MET: explain how weather affects your life; use phrasal verbs

Video

A Watch the video and check (✓) *True* or *False*.

	True	False
1. Erosion of the British coastline has been going on for about one hundred years.	☐	☐
2. Most of the money is spent on rock bolts and new sand.	☐	☐
3. Paper is a good way to fill in the cracks.	☐	☐
4. Global warming is causing sea levels to rise.	☐	☐
5. In only thirty years, they have lost more than half of the salt marsh.	☐	☐
6. Salt marshes are growing and spreading inland.	☐	☐

B Answer the questions based on what these people say in the video.

1. Do you think John Riby is in favor of or against defending the coastline? Why?

2. Does Graham Game think that losing the salt marsh in Essex is a major or minor problem? Why?

OUTCOME MET: make inferences based on information you have learned

Writing

The expression "March goes in like a lion and out like a lamb" couldn't have been truer for Fiona this year. It was March 3, and she had plans to go out with her sister. She looked out the window and noticed that it was snowing quite hard. The wind was howling like a wolf. She opened the door and tried to run to her car, but it was too icy and she slipped! Frustrated, she ran back inside. She tried to call her sister, but the connection got cut off after one ring. Luckily, her heat was still working. She decided to relax and read a book on the couch. Under her blanket, she was as snug as a bug in a rug. The storm lasted all day and knocked down some trees. Finally, her phone started working, and she was able to talk to her sister. They rescheduled their outing for March 24, which happened to be a bright and sunny day. The weather was as mild as a lamb!

A Underline the phrasal verbs in the story. Then write down the similes from the story.

1. ______________________
2. ______________________
3. ______________________

B Now write three similes comparing people and the weather to the animals pictured. Here are some words you may want to use: *cold, mild, angry, tired, sweet, wild, quiet, happy*.

Example: *Ted was as hungry as a lion. / The storm was like an angry lion.*

1. ______________________
2. ______________________
3. ______________________

C Write a creative story about someone who has an interesting experience or adventure because of the weather. Include two of the similes you wrote for Exercise **B** (or new ones). Be sure to use at least two of the following phrasal verbs in your story: *give up, look after, put on, take off, look for, clean up, pick up, die down, cheer up, wake up, run away, warm up*.

____

____

____

____

____

OUTCOMES MET: understand and use similes; use phrasal verbs

Reading

Changing Rains

Global warming could make wet places wetter...

At times in history, changes in climate have caused civilizations to fall. Climate scientists believe that major changes in rainfall were to blame for the decline of at least four major groups. These groups are the Akkad Empire in modern-day Iraq (4,300 years ago), the Old Kingdom of Egypt (same time), the Tiwanacu civilization of the Andes Mountains (1100 CE), and the Maya civilization of Mexico (800 CE).

The rainfall changes that brought down these early civilizations happened because of natural climate shifts of unknown causes. By contrast, climate change that happens because of increasing levels of greenhouse gas has a known cause: human activity. But the effects could be the same if global warming continues to impact the earth's precipitation.[1]

Warm air holds more water vapor. So a hotter world is a world where the atmosphere has more moisture. This might not mean more rain. In fact, most scientists believe that total precipitation will increase only a little. The changes are expected to happen where the rain falls.

A good general rule of thumb, says scientist Isaac Held, is that "wet areas are going to get wetter, and dry areas drier." Since higher temperatures cause water to evaporate[2] more, even areas that still receive the same amount of precipitation will be more likely to experience droughts.[3]

... and dry places drier.

Meanwhile, when it does rain, it will likely come down stronger and increase the chance of flooding. A recent United Nations report says that "heavy precipitation events are projected to become more frequent." Between 1996 and 2005, there were twice as many inland flood disasters as in the thirty years between 1950 and 1980.

Experts say that we may not know how climate change really affects rainfall until the middle of this century. But some facts are known. Between 1925 and 1999, the area between 40 and 70 degrees north latitude got rainier. During those same years, the area between 0 and 30 degrees north latitude grew drier. The island of Cyprus, for example, has become so dry that it had to start shipping water from Greece in the summer of 2008.

Will the rainfall changes of the future affect societies as severely as some of the changes of the past? To look at one example, the American Southwest has had droughts severe enough to destroy local populations. (It is believed that one huge drought in the region caused the decline of the Anasazi civilization at the end of the 13th century.) Nowadays, of course, people are better at water management than they used to be. But how will that hold up against the increasing dryness that climate change causes?

"We do not know, because we have not been at this point before," said Richard Seager, an expert on the Southwest's climate history. "But as man changes the climate, we may be about to find out."

[1] **precipitation** moisture, such as rain and snow, that falls to the earth
[2] **evaporate** the process that turns water into vapor in the air
[3] **drought** a long period of no rain

A Choose the correct answer based on the reading.

1. Scientists believe that in the past, changes in ______ may have caused some civilizations to decline.
   a. rainfall b. temperature c. location
2. As the world gets hotter, it creates more ______ in the atmosphere.
   a. wind b. moisture c. storms
3. Because of climate change, the level of precipitation in an area that is already dry will probably ______.
   a. increase b. decrease c. stay the same
4. There were twice as many floods between 1996 and 2005 as there were between ______.
   a. 1950 and 1980 b. 800 and 1100 CE c. 1925 and 1999
5. One advantage that modern societies have over past civilizations is better ______.
   a. governments b. droughts c. water management

B Answer the questions with your own ideas.

1. The statement "wet areas are going to get wetter, and dry areas drier" is called a "rule of thumb." Define in your own words what a "rule of thumb" is.

   ____

2. What inference can you make about the location of the island of Cyprus based on the description?

   ____

3. In what ways do you think people are better at water management than in previous societies?

   ____

4. What can you infer will happen to the climate in the American Southwest if the predictions in the article are true?

   ____

OUTCOME MET: make inferences based on information you have learned

C Think about the climate where you live in terms of rainfall. Based on the information in the article, how will climate change affect your area? Write a paragraph describing how climate might change and how it would affect you.

____

____

____

____

____

____

____

____

____

____

____

OUTCOME MET: explain how weather affects your life

Outcomes

A Answer the questions in complete sentences.

1. What is the weather like during different times of the year where you live? ____________________
2. Are there times when you cannot do certain activities because of weather? Explain how the weather in each season affects you. ____________________

How did you do?: On a scale of 1–5 (with 5 being the best), how well did you **explain how weather affects your life?** ____

B Answer the questions based on the dialogue in Exercise **A** on page 67. Use complete sentences.

1. Do Marcos and his sister get along? How do you know?
2. Where do you think Julia lives? What gives you that idea?
3. Where do you think Marcos lives? ____________________
4. Do you think that Julia will be happy after she arrives in Marcos's city? Why or why not?

How did you do?: On a scale of 1–5, how well did you **make inferences based on information you have learned?** ____

C Complete the chart with a simile that goes with the given meaning or the meaning of the given simile.

Simile	Meaning
1. He's as subtle as an elephant.	1.
2.	2. She's really tall.
3. He's as cold as ice.	3.
4.	4. It's extremely warm today.
5. She sings like a bird.	5.

How did you do?: On a scale of 1–5, how well did you **understand and use similes?** ____

D Write sentences using the phrasal verbs in parentheses.

1. (give up) ____________________
2. (look after) ____________________
3. (cut off) ____________________
4. (take off) ____________________

How did you do?: On a scale of 1–5, how well did you **use phrasal verbs?** ____

12 What's Your Game?

Vocabulary and Grammar

Unit 12 Outcomes

- use reported speech to explain what someone else said
- evaluate the relationship between activities and personal qualities
- pace yourself as you write a timed essay
- use an outline to support a presentation or essay

A Match the word on the left with its opposite meaning on the right.

1. defend ______
2. opponent ______
3. achieve ______
4. in shape ______
5. obsessed ______
6. commitment ______

a. unfit
b. fail
c. attack
d. ally
e. uninterested
f. indifference

B Complete the sentences with vocabulary words from the box. One will not be used. Then rewrite the exact quotes using reported speech.

beat	championship	defend	in shape	obsessed	opponents

1. Isla said, "I am ____________ with professional tennis."
   ____
2. Charlotte asked, "Can you get me tickets to the ____________ tennis match this year?"
   ____
3. Jae asked, "Is that how you stay ____________, Isla?"
   ____
4. Isla said, "Yes. Charlotte and I play tennis together often."
   ____
5. Jae asked, "Would you want to play doubles against Ramon and me? We are strong ____________."
   ____
6. Isla said, "Definitely! With Charlotte as my partner, we'll surely ____________ you!"
   ____

OUTCOME MET: use reported speech to explain what someone else said

C Answer the questions with complete sentences.

1. What makes someone a good **coach**?
   ____
2. What makes someone a good or bad **opponent**?
   ____
3. Think about someone you know who is **obsessed** with a sport or activity. What is he or she like?
   ____
4. Think about someone you know who is **in shape**. What is he or she like?
   ____

OUTCOME MET: evaluate the relationship between activities and personal qualities

D Rewrite what these people say using reported speech and the word in parentheses.

Example: The coach (encourage): "You should work hard to achieve your goals."
The coach encouraged me to work hard in order to achieve my goals.

1. Jia (explain): "Training for a marathon is a big commitment."
____
____
____
____

2. Gavi (beg): "Please let me watch another hour of television!"
____
____
____
____

3. Marcos (promise): "I will teach Samuel how to fish this weekend."
____
____
____
____

4. Amelia (say): "My biggest motivation for cycling is to seek adventure."
____
____
____
____

OUTCOME MET: use reported speech to explain what someone else said

Video

A Watch the video. Write the letter of the correct answers to the questions.

1. Alain's climbs are very dangerous because he climbs ______.
   a. with only his climbing shoes and chalk
   b. without permits or chalk
   c. without rope or climbing shoes

2. He has damaged his ______ due to climbing and can't straighten them normally.
   a. fingers
   b. feet
   c. knees

3. A typical climb takes place in a ______.
   a. low-key urban zone
   b. quiet suburban area
   c. busy, city neighborhood

4. Alain began the sport by climbing ______.
   a. buildings in his hometown
   b. in an indoor gym
   c. rocks in the mountains near his home

B Read the text from the video. Then answer the questions with complete sentences. *Whether he is on a mountain or on a building, even if he thinks he might fall, he carries on, because, as he says, "When you are facing a problem where your life is in danger, there is only one option."*

1. Rewrite what Alain says above using reported speech. _______________
____

2. What does Alain mean when he says that there is only one option? _______________
____

3. What personal qualities does Alain possess that allow him to climb buildings? _______________
____

4. Are you similar to Alain or different? How? Compare yourself to him. _______________
____

Writing

A Choose one of the images. Then answer the questions using your own ideas.

1. What is the person's name? ______________________
2. What activity is he or she doing in the picture? ______________________
3. What qualities does he or she possess that make this person good at the activity?

   ____
4. What is this person like? ______________________
5. Write two other interesting facts about the person.

   ____

   ____

B You are going to write a short biography of the person whose information you invented in Exercise **A**. Your biography will provide information about what this person is like and what activities he or she does. First, create an outline about the person based on the information in Exercise **A**.

1. (intro: main idea) ______________________
   A. ______________________
   B. ______________________
2. (body: main idea) ______________________
   A. ______________________
   B. ______________________
3. (conclusion: main idea) ______________________
   A. ______________________
   B. ______________________

OUTCOME MET: use an outline to support a presentation or essay

C You are now going to write about the person in the photo, using the outline from Exercise **B**. Use a timer and give yourself twenty minutes to write your biographical sketch on a separate piece of paper. Be creative!

OUTCOME MET: pace yourself as you write a timed essay

Reading

Paddleboard Racing: Surfing the Hard Way

Paddleboard racer Jamie Mitchell

The open ocean, a long floating board, an athlete in a wetsuit[1]... for traditional surfers, the only thing missing from a scene like that would be high, rolling waves to ride as they guide the board toward the shore. But for paddleboard racers like Jamie Mitchell, huge waves are the last thing they want to see.

Paddleboard racing might be the hardest water sport that no one knows about. Like surfing, paddleboard racing uses a long narrow board that slices through the ocean's choppy waters. But instead of steering the board while standing, paddleboard racers kneel or lie on their stomachs and use their arms to paddle.

Although surfing lying down might sound like an easier way to hit the waves, it actually requires much more physical strength and is a lot harder on a person's body. Athletes don't ride waves in paddleboard racing like they do in surfing. Instead, they often have to move parallel to or directly at the rolling waves. It's harder to balance the board from a low position, and racers are always at risk of tipping over. Also, the constant rubbing of the board against a racer's wet feet, knees, and stomach causes painful rashes and blisters[2] on the skin.

But that doesn't keep paddleboard racers like Australian Jamie Mitchell from training up to three times a day, six days a week. And the hard work has paid off. Mitchell recently won the 51.5-kilometer (32-mile) Moloka'i to Oahu Paddleboard Race for the tenth straight year, making him the sport's unofficial champion.

The race goes through the Moloka'i Channel, which passes between the Hawaiian islands of Moloka'i and Oahu. The waters there are known for being very rough and fast-moving. Mitchell called the 2009 race "the toughest of the last three or four years for me." He still went on to win that race, plus the next two after that.

Possibly the biggest challenge of paddleboard racing is that it doesn't pay well. Mitchell needs other jobs in order to pay his bills. Fortunately, he's also one of the world's best athletes in two other sports: big-wave surfing and stand-up paddling.

But Jamie Mitchell considers himself a paddleboard racer first. He's not motivated by money but instead by being the best he can. "There are very few people who are capable of investing as much of their life in something or sacrificing as much as it takes to win the Moloka'i," Mitchell says. "And because of that, they can't understand why it's such an accomplishment."

[1] **wetsuit** clothing that keeps water-sports athletes warm
[2] **rashes and blisters** places where the skin is injured from rubbing

A Answer the questions in complete sentences.

1. What is paddleboard racing?
2. How would you describe Jamie Mitchell?
3. Why is the Moloka'i to Oahu race so difficult?
4. What other water sports does Jamie Mitchell do?
5. Can Jamie support himself on the money he wins paddleboard racing?
6. What do you think his motivation is?
7. Had you ever heard of paddleboard racing before reading this article?
8. Would you be willing to work so hard at a sport that not many people know about?
9. Why do you think he's interested in a sport that doesn't pay very well?
10. What is something you do just because you love to do it?

OUTCOME MET: evaluate the relationship between activities and personal qualities

B Write a paragraph in your own words summarizing the article about Jamie Mitchell. Use a timer and allow yourself exactly ten minutes to write it.

OUTCOME MET: pace yourself as you write a timed essay

Outcomes

A Change the statements to reported speech. Use *asked, told, encouraged, begged*, or *explained*.

1. The coach said to the team, "Do your best on the field today."
______
2. Hannah said to her dad, "Please let me borrow the car tonight."
______
3. Micah said to his friend, "The reason I'm late is because I couldn't find my phone."
______
4. Terrance said to his students, "Study for the test."
______

How did you do?: On a scale of 1–5 (with 5 being the best), how well did you **use reported speech to explain what someone else said?** ______

B Choose three of the sports or activities listed below. Then write a sentence describing what kind of a person it would take to be good at each activity.

auto racing **bowling** **boxing** **chess** **dancing** **golf** **swimming** **yoga**

Sport/activity	Sentence
1.	
2.	
3.	

How did you do?: On a scale of 1–5, how well did you **evaluate the relationship between activities and personal qualities?** ______

C Write a paragraph about a popular activity or sport that you like to do. Give yourself exactly five minutes to write. Include an introduction, main idea, supporting details, and a conclusion.

______
______
______
______
______

How did you do?: On a scale of 1–5, how well did you **pace yourself as you wrote a timed essay?** ______

D On a separate piece of paper, write an outline to show how your essay above is organized.

How did you do?: On a scale of 1–5, how well did you **use an outline to support a presentation or essay?** ______

10–12 Review

Vocabulary Review

A Match the verb to its definition.

1. ______ to permit or accept something you don't believe in	a.	achieve
2. ______ to win against someone in a competition	b.	concentrate
3. ______ to influence something to happen	c.	recover
4. ______ to wait a little while before speaking or acting	d.	beat
5. ______ to pay close attention to something	e.	affect
6. ______ to protect somebody or something	f.	refuse
7. ______ to feel sorry about something that happened	g.	defend
8. ______ to feel well again	h.	tolerate
9. ______ to succeed in something after working hard at it	i.	regret
10. ______ to say no	j.	hesitate

B Answer the questions using words from the box. Not all words are used.

assess	**coach**	**effect**	**intervene**	**mind**
championship	**consider**	**frigid**	**mild**	**postpone**

1. Which two words involve *thinking about a problem*? ____________________
2. Which two words describe *weather*? ____________________
3. What is another word for *delay*? ____________________
4. Which word best describes a competition to find the best team? ____________________
5. What word completes these expressions: *make up your* ____ or *speak your* ____? ____________________

C You are a coach of a soccer team that has just won a championship. Complete the interview by answering the questions. Use words from the box.

beat	**commitment**	**figure out**	**in shape**	**motivation**	**regret**
coach	**consider**	**give up**	**intervene**	**opponent**	**tolerate**

Interviewer: What was the motivation behind your success this season?

Coach: (1) ____________________

Interviewer: How does the team stay in shape?

Coach: (2) ____________________

Interviewer: In the championship game, you were losing until the last few minutes when Pierre Ducout scored the final two goals. Explain how you won.

Coach: (3) ____________________

Interviewer: Do you have any regrets about this season?

Coach: (4) ____________________

Grammar Review

A Complete the sentences with the correct form of the verb in parentheses.

Example: I am at work. If I were (be) at the gym right now, I would run (run) on the treadmill.

1. José might buy a bike. If he ______________ (get) one, he ______________ (ride) it to school.
2. I don't live near school. If I ______________ (live) closer, I ______________ (walk) to class.
3. Lila is busy this weekend. If she ______________ (have) any free time, she ______________ (go) to yoga.
4. Xavier isn't a good swimmer. If he ______________ (swim) well, he ______________ (join) the swim team.
5. We're studying now. If we ______________ (finish) studying by five, we ______________ (cook) dinner.

B Report what Kal said to you using verbs like *tell, explain, say, encourage, ask,* etc.

1. "You should study on Saturday, not tonight."
____
2. "Please change your mind and come to the movies with us."
____
3. "We are going to see the new Brad Pitt movie. It's supposed to be great."
____
4. "Did you know that the actor had to train four hours a day for the role?"
____

C Complete the text messages with the correct phrasal verbs from the box. Some will not be used.

check in	found out	look into	take off
cut off	give up	picked up	woke up

I am at the airport. I just (1) ______________ that our flight is delayed. ☹

Oh good. My alarm didn't go off so I (2) ______________ late.

Don't rush! The weather is bad—the winds have (3) ______________.

What time do you think the plane will (4) ______________?

Hold on. I will (5) ______________ it.

Ok. I can't wait to get away. It will be nice to be somewhere warm! ☺

Definitely! They said that we will have to wait at least two more hours.

I just got to the airport. I need to (6) ______________. See you soon!

D Imagine that you could spend six months anywhere in the world and learn something new. Describe where you would go, what you would do there, and explain why.

____

____

Review Surveys

Unit 7: Getting around

Ask your classmates the following survey questions. Keep track of their responses in the chart below.

1. How do you commute to school?
2. Would you rather take a bus or a train to travel across the country, and why?
3. What is the most reliable form of transportation?

Name	Question 1	Question 2	Question 3

Unit 8: Follow the rules

Ask your classmates the following survey questions. Keep track of their responses in the chart below.

1. What class could you have taken if you weren't studying English?
2. What should students do to be respectful to teachers?
3. What should be the consequences of cheating on a test?

Name	Question 1	Question 2	Question 3

Unit 9: Animal life

Ask your classmates the following survey questions. Keep track of their responses in the chart below.

1. Do you think it's cruel to capture animals to put in zoos?
2. What wild animal do you wish could be domesticated?
3. Should animals be hunted for food?

Name	Question 1	Question 2	Question 3

Unit 10: Your choice

Ask your classmates the following survey questions. Keep track of their responses in the chart below.

1. If you could be a famous celebrity or a great athlete, which would you choose?
2. What is a decision that you regret to this day?
3. Is it ever a good idea to hesitate before you make a decision?

Name	Question 1	Question 2	Question 3

Unit 11: Hot and cold

Ask your classmates the following survey questions. Keep track of their responses in the chart below.

1. What kind of weather do you think is the hardest to put up with?
2. How do you warm yourself up on a very cold day?
3. If you didn't have time to study English and do your favorite hobby, which would you give up?

Name	Question 1	Question 2	Question 3

Unit 12: Play the game

Ask your classmates the following survey questions. Keep track of their responses in the chart below.

1. What qualities must someone have to be an athlete?
2. If you play sports or games, is it good to be obsessed about winning?
3. What is something a relative, a friend, or a coach has said to help you achieve a goal?

Name	Question 1	Question 2	Question 3

Survey Result Reports

Record the results of your surveys as summaries. Use the phrases below to help you.

The majority of people …	**Quite a few people …**	**Hardly any of the people …**
Most people …	**About half of the people …**	**Almost no one …**

Unit 7: Getting around ______________________________

Unit 8: Follow the rules ______________________________

Unit 9: Animal life ______________________________

Unit 10: Your choice ______________________________

Unit 11: Hot and cold ______________________________

Unit 12: Play the game ______________________________

Review Puzzle

Units 7–9

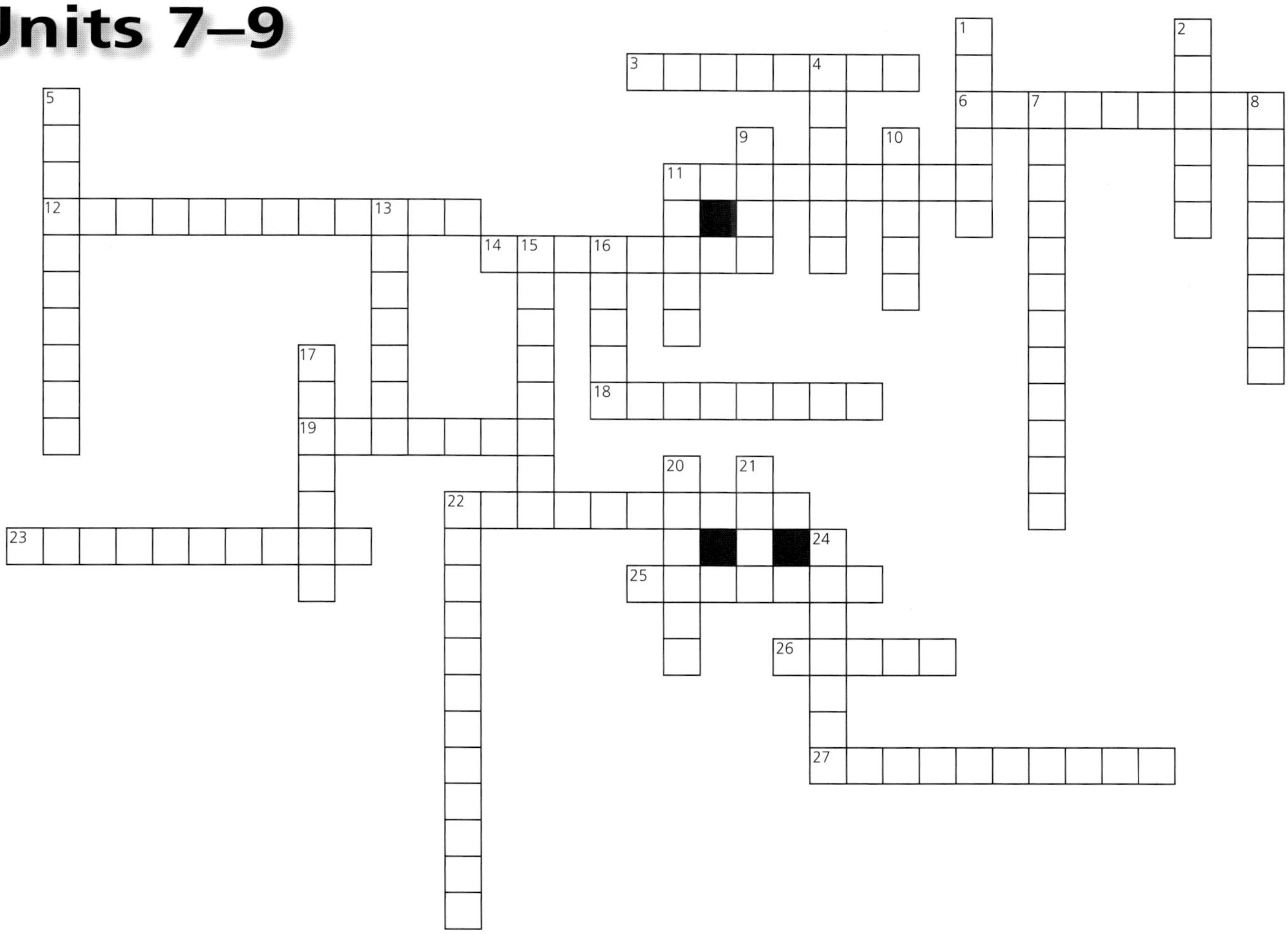

ACROSS

3. the time when a lot of people are commuting (2 words)
6. I ___ have been texting while driving. I'm sorry. (2 words)
11. to show disapproval
12. results of an action
14. My dog ___ (find) by my neighbor last night. (2 words)
18. another word for *dependable*
19. Wild animals ___ (keep) in cages at the zoo. (2 words)
22. polite and considerate
23. Zoos try to protect ___ species.
25. another word for *catch*
26. Sarika ___ have gone to class, but I'm not sure.
27. The teacher does not allow ___ behavior in class.

DOWN

1. A taxi is fast but the subway is ___.
2. to act against bad behavior
4. another word for *choice*
5. The train arrives more ___ than the bus; it's always on time
7. hard to fight against; overpowering
8. to move something from one place to another
9. the opposite of *domesticated*
10. to feel like you belong (2 words)
11. the opposite of *kind*
13. the trip between home and school or work
15. Biking is ___ taking the bus. We'll arrive at the same time. (3 words)
16. An express bus makes ___ stops than the local bus.
17. the opposite of roomy
20. to try to hurt someone
21. to pursue an animal for food
22. There are ___ on texting while driving.
24. The horse can jump over the fence. It has been ___.

Review Puzzle

Units 10–12

ACROSS

5. to accept something
7. We won't go outside until the winds ___. (2 words)
11. someone who trains others to play a sport
14. If the sun comes out, we ___ (walk) to the beach. (2 words)
15. I would study at least three hours ___ I were you.
17. always thinking about something
20. to protect
21. freezing
22. to feel sorry about how something turned out
24. Your brain is able to ___ information faster than a computer.
26. a result of an action
27. My call got ___ when I entered the tunnel. (2 words)
28. The game has been ___ because of rain.

DOWN

1. to get involved
2. My friend ___ (beg) me to go with her to Spain.
3. warm and pleasant
4. logical or reasonable
6. the other team or player in a game
8. If I had enough money, I ___ (go) to Brazil. (2 words)
9. to take care of someone (2 words)
10. We can still win the game. Don't ___! (2 words)
12. I was going to play soccer but I changed my ___.
13. Sam ___ (tell) me he got a job.
16. to discover the solution to a problem (2 words)
18. to defeat
19. If I ___ (be) at the gym right now, I would lift weights.
23. another word for *judge*
25. the opposite of *accept*